*Praise for Laura*

# CLAIMING GROUND

"Luminous. . . . Can be savored for the lyricism of its language, its insight into a distinct American region and a meditation on physical work and the role it played in one woman's life."
—*Minneapolis Star Tribune*

"Part lyrical remembrance of a deeply intense relationship with nature in a sweepingly majestic landscape, part unswerving self-analysis, *Claiming Ground* delivers both beauty and unabashed reflection."
—*BookPage*

"Bell loves the solitude for its grandeur and for connecting her to the wildlife, all of which she renders in a luminous and flinty prose attuned to the country."
—*The Free Lance-Star* (Fredericksburg, Virginia)

"Unique and engaging. . . . Well worth reading."
—*San Francisco Chronicle*

"If you couldn't put down Elizabeth Gilbert's *Eat, Pray, Love,* you must go out right this minute and buy Laura Bell's *Claiming Ground.* . . . Worth is rarely the measure of a book's success, but if ever a memoir deserved to be a bestseller, *Claiming Ground* surely does. . . . Brave and honest. . . . Endlessly inventive."
—*Nashville Scene*

"Quietly powerful. . . . Bell's writing elegantly balances pain and love, solitude and family ties, finding solace both in human relationships and in relationships to animals and the Western landscape. Big and openhearted like the Wyoming sky, this memoir is a pleasure to read."
—*Sacramento Book Review*

"Brings a unique point of view—and tremendous writing talent—to [the American West]. . . . A portrait of the inextricable link between a person and a place."      —*Salt Lake City Weekly*

"Bell tenderly writes about the people in her life with grace and reverence, never sacrificing honesty."      —*Billings Gazette*

"Has brought more than one reader to tears. . . . Vivid."
—*Cody Enterprise* (Wyoming)

"A heart-wrenching ode to the rough, enormous beauty of the Western landscape."      —The Nature Conservancy

"Bell's gift for observation, generous analysis, and her ability to turn a place and people into words are uncommon—traits she shares with the likes of Norman Maclean and Wallace Stegner, but few others. . . . [A] fine book."
—*Metro Pulse* (Knoxville, Tennessee)

"Open, honest, strong and unflinching."
—*The Durango Herald* (Colorado)

"A wonderfully written, refreshing story." —William Kittredge

"Intriguing and eloquent, by turns guarded then vulnerable, and always written with honesty and keen observation, Laura Bell's *Claiming Ground* merges exquisitely the human condition of wonder, celebration, fear, and longing with the Western landscape that so arouses and nurtures these same senses."

—Rick Bass

"Deeply felt. . . . Each twist of the story [is] viscerally evoked by Bell's wrenching, raw, and honest prose."  —*Orion Magazine*

"[Bell] describes a world that most would have trouble imagining—what the inside of a sheepwagon looks like, how to spot a cow in labor, what little luxuries fit best inside saddlebags. . . . Bell watches the land with an attentiveness gained from years of scanning the horizon for wayward sheep, and she captures its sights and sounds with startling beauty."

—*High Country News*

# LAURA BELL

# CLAIMING GROUND

Laura Bell's work has been published in several collections, and from the Wyoming Arts Council she has received two literature fellowships as well as the Neltje Blanchan Memorial Award and the Frank Nelson Doubleday Memorial Award. She lives with her husband and dogs in Wyoming and Florida.

# CLAIMING GROUND

## LAURA BELL

VINTAGE BOOKS

A DIVISION OF RANDOM HOUSE, INC.

NEW YORK

For Virginia and Wayne Bell, Amy Little Bey,
and Jennifer Nicole Little (1981–1999)

FIRST VINTAGE BOOKS EDITION, APRIL 2011

*Copyright © 2010 by Laura Bell*

Grateful acknowledgment is made to the following for permission to reprint
previously published material:
Ahsahta Press: Excerpt from "Probably She Is a River" from
*To Touch the Water* by Gretel Ehrlich (Boise, ID: Ahsahta Press, 1981).
Reprinted by permission of Ahsahta Press.
The Estate of Robert W. Service: Excerpt from "The Cremation of Sam McGee"
from *The Spell of the Yukon and Other Verses* by Robert W. Service
(New York: Barse & Hopkins, 1907). Reprinted by permission of
William Krasilovsky on behalf of the Estate of Robert W. Service.
Hal Leonard Corporation: Excerpt from "Remember Me (When the Candle Lights
Are Gleaming)," words and music by Scott Wiseman, copyright © 1946
by Universal—Songs of Polygram International, Inc. Copyright renewed.
All rights reserved. Reprinted by permission of
Hal Leonard Corporation.

The Library of Congress has cataloged the Knopf edition as follows:
Bell, Laura, 1954–
Claiming ground / by Laura Bell.
p. cm.
1. Bell, Laura, 1954–. 2. Ranch life—Wyoming.
3. Wyoming—Social life and customs. 4. Sheepherding—Wyoming.
5. Ranching—Wyoming. 6. Ranches—Wyoming. 7. Wyoming—History, Local.
8. Young women—Wyoming—Biography. 9. Wyoming—Biography. I. Title.
F765.22.B45A3 2010
978.7'033092—dc22
[B] 2009029644

Vintage ISBN: 978-0-307-47464-3

*Book design by Soonyoung Kwon*

www.vintagebooks.com

Printed in the United States of America
10  9  8  7  6  5  4  3  2  1

*. . . every heart to love will come, but like a refugee.*

—LEONARD COHEN, *ANTHEM*

# CONTENTS

# CLAIMING GROUND

# MIGRATION

The sheepwagon door stands open to the early dawn. There are times when sleeping inside feels little different than sleeping out like the dogs curled in their scratched beds or the sheep planted against one another across the rise. There's a blanket, a curve of metal roof, a shelf of books above the bed. From up in the McCullough Peaks a lone coyote yips, sharp and high. There comes an answer, closer, the voices halting at first, then unraveling slowly into a mad chorus of wavering howls. Through the doorway, I see the dogs appear and settle their haunches into the dirt. They watch out over the land, their ears shifting to the cries like antennae. When silence returns, they lower themselves to the ground, still listening.

Under the covers, my hands are still against my bones, the edge of longing too great to name or call up. I wish for a fire to be lit in the iron stove by the door. I wish for the smell of coffee, a cup warm in my hands, a voice to say my name.

A dawn wind rustles loose tin and whispers through stiff sprigs of sage, their seedheads quivering against the wind for as far as I can see into the murky light and beyond, into the empty miles. East, across the Big Horn Basin, the horizon of mountains bears up the salmon wash of morning.

There were nine men herding for the ranch, each with at least a thousand head of sheep in his care. Red, Grady, Murdi, Maurice, Rudy, Ed, Doug, Albert and others that came and went, all crossing the days, one by one, from their calendars. They smelled of sheep tallow, woodsmoke and kerosene, and sometimes of whiskey seeping through their pores. Some of them brought a rare beauty and grace to their work. Others, psychotic or drunk, herded because they couldn't find a place among people. In the three years I herded, I came to understand they were often one and the same. They wove the line between sacred and profane, never staying much to center. I came to them the observer, the adventurer, thinking myself different and holding myself apart. I came to them a young woman among old men, but what we had in common was that line.

Across the rangelands of northwest Wyoming, they herded, headed slowly for higher ground, for tender grass and air that held some scrap of moisture. Through brief summer months they hung suspended at the top of the Big Horns. Between timberline and sky, drifts of snow gave way to pools of wild sweet arnica and sheep spread across the earth like clouds run to ground. Beneath early snows of September, the herders retreated, following the sheep down to where the range was more dirt than grass and the slanting sun would give them a brief reprieve on winter. For ten months of every year the sheep and the herders moved across this corner of the map, rising and falling, their tracks a waltz driven by time and weather and the sureness of both.


The men were cared for by John Lewis Hopkin, the grandson of the ranch's original owner, and Sterling, the man who helped him during the years I herded. They tended the camps and nursed the men's eccentricities, becoming for them the one line of communication with the outside world. Once a week, they'd drive out to each camp, hauling horse oats, groceries, water, mail, rifle shells, and gossip from town. The herders would try to make this visit last as long as possible. Rudy would offer up Dutch-oven biscuits and a long list of complaints, Maurice, a pot of pinto beans with ham and tortillas rolled by hand on top of the wood stove. Some would string it out with a search for some phantom sick lamb or ewe.

Grady would have coffee, sometimes an excellent mutton stew, and, in the months he was sober, good conversation and a quick wit. As for me, I was a listener and a woman among men. This alone was often enough.

Once a week the camps would be tended. After the grind of the pickup engine faded in the distance, there'd be only the sound of sheep, of wind, of our own voices speaking out loud.

The ranch was sprawling, reaching seventy miles across the Big Horn Basin and spilling up into the high sagebrush benches of southern Montana. It was called the Lewis Ranch and had been established by Claude Lewis, the grandson of Mormon pioneers, from the misfortunes of homesteaders during the destitute thirties. At its peak it had run twenty thousand ewes in twenty bands, but over the years half the sheep were replaced with cattle and cowboys who demanded less patience and attention. All the sheep would have been sold but for the tenaciousness of John, the only sheepman in the family once his grandfather was gone.

The skeleton of the ranch was stitched together from smaller farms and ranches along the Shoshone River and the Big Horn, with their headwaters high in the Wind and Absaroka Ranges, and the meager creeks—Crooked, Gypsum, Dry, Whistle and Pryor—that channeled spring melts and infrequent rains. These places held the lambing sheds, the calving corrals, the plowed fields, and they had machinery and telephones, hot showers, and kitchen tables with the imprints of forearms worn into their vinyl coverings. These were tired places with faded paint, and they worked hard for a living, but still they were connected to the tangled life of the small towns of Lovell, Cowley, Deaver and Byron. And to the Mormon Church and to bars, to Saturday night dances, to the string of human interactions on any given day that a person can take for granted.

For just two months a year, the sheepherders would be exposed to the edges of this life, and even that exacted a heavy toll. In early February, the sheep would be trailed in from their winter ranges to the Lovell lambing sheds, where they were sheared in preparation for the lambing season. The herders' wagons would be lined up side by side along the east edge of the pens, backed up to the fence and facing the cottonwood bottom of the Big Horn River.

With neighbors only feet away and without miles to buffer them from town's ragged temptations, many of those quiet men unraveled. It might begin with a swig of wine offered by the Mexican shearing crew or a half pint of whiskey pulled from a ranch hand's pocket. Otherwise quiet men would grow loud and then disappear. Some, the younger of the old men, planned for it with enthusiasm, counting the days until they were free to go, slicking back their hair and believing that love might be found on a barstool. Days or weeks later, a rattling car would drop them off, stumbling, at their wagon, or they'd walk the highway home in the late night. A year's wages could be lost in that brief, bright sparkling. The Medicine Wheel Bar, the Cactus, the Oasis, the Shoshone, the Waterhole. Drinks were bought for the bar, money given away to strangers, saddles and rifles hocked or sold. When they reached hard bottom, out of money or health or both, they would return as quiet men again, content with the peculiar confines of their lives.

The ranch's spring ranges pushed west to the McCullough Peaks and the foothills of the volcanic Absaroka Range, north along the Polecat Bench and up into the Pryor Gap country of the Dryhead Ranch, east to the uplifted limestone slabs of the Big Horn Mountains. Straight out of the sheds, the lambs too young to trail, the sheep were loaded into semis and trucked out to the spring ranges. Days before, John and Sterling would haul the herders and wagons out into the hills, miles apart from one another, and leave them to wait alone and afoot for their sheep and horse to arrive. There, the spare rangelands are brightening with new growth: Wyoming big sage, blue gramma, needle and thread, Indian ricegrass, and, scattered among the grasses, delicate evening primrose, copper mallow, and Indian paintbrush in clumps of red, fluorescent pink, and magenta. For some, these are days of sobering up, of nursing the alcoholic shakes with strong coffee, a six-pack of beer, and the company of their dogs. For all, this time seems a true reflection of the distance between them and the world.

Sheepwagons are set and leveled where the view of the country is long and generous and includes a pond or creek where the sheep can water. Like tiny ships at sea, the wagons are built to provide sturdy shelter from the elements and to hold its contents securely in place across the miles. Their rounded roofs are metal or canvas stretched across wooden bows. Above the wagon tongue is a door, split, and through it to either side a wood cookstove and cabinets. Benches run along the sides with storage beneath, and reaching across the back is a bed with more cabinets beneath and a small window behind. From the framework of the bed, a bit of plywood can be pulled out like a kitchen cutting board to serve as the table.

On this first trip out in the spring, the tender leaves the herder with a well-stocked camp and drives away. A few days, maybe a week later, the rumbling of trucks breaks the silence and along with the rumbling the rising, bleating clamor of ewes and lambs. When the trucks stop and the dust settles, metal ramps are pulled down and the ewes and lambs spill to the ground and spread and roil through the tender new grass. For the rest of that day, the herder will walk the edges of this chaos with dogs and horse, bumping strays back to center until the reunions between ewes and lambs eventually bring quiet to the waning light.

The sheep give the herders purpose again, placing them back in a world where they belong. But for those few days without sheep, their world is made up of thin air and silence, a blank slate that had sent more than one new man walking back to town.

In the early fall, after the lambs have been shipped to market, the ewes are trailed from the mountain with bitter winds sweeping at their backsides and doubled up into winter bands of two thousand or more, with the bucks thrown in for breeding. There on the low-elevation winter ranges, they paw the snow for shrubby winterfat and eat the tips from sage. The toughest of the herders stay with their sheep through the hard months of November, December, and January, gathering dogs to their beds when the temperatures fall to twenty and forty below, sleeping with eggs and potatoes under the covers to keep them from freezing in the night. At Thanksgiving, John brings a turkey dinner. At Christmas, a ham and a brand-new Pendleton wool shirt, gifts from the ranch.

As a young woman, I found my way into the middle of these lives. I'd come to Wyoming, twenty-two and fresh out of college, to travel with my sister and her five-month-old son while her husband worked on a paleontological dig at Natural Trap Cave on the lower reaches of the northern Big Horn Mountains. We'd camped into Montana's Pryor Mountains, the Pryor Gap, and on up north to Glacier National Park but were drawn back to the ragtag, anything-goes dig site on Little Mountain, where tents and clothes and Buddhist prayer flags all flapped in the wind. I developed a crush on the head of the dig, Miles, a sinewy paleontologist who quoted poetry and sometimes brushed his teeth with a shot of Jack Daniels in the morning. On the day before I was to head back east with my sister, Miles took us up the mountain toward the Medicine Wheel to picnic with an old sheepherder, Doug, who worked for the Lewis Ranch.

He was camped at the Little Headquarters, a low-slung, one-room log cabin, with an attached shed where he kept a circus of goats, dogs and horses. As a child I'd hidden within the pages of books, crafting my own particular fantasy of a life lived out, with mountains, horses, a cabin, animals that I alone could befriend. I later learned that most of the sheepherders, including Doug, lived this reclusive life to save themselves from the raging alcoholism that pursued them in town, but to me it seemed idyllic. I longed for it, so much so that when I went with Doug to retrieve canned drinks chilling in his spring, the words came blurting out, "Can I stay here? Do you need any help?"

Doug's cabin was one of eight line camps scattered across the midelevation benches of Little Mountain, remote country where the sheep would be held for several weeks between the drying of the spring ranges in summer's heat and the opening of the higher altitude Big Horn National Forest grazing allotments. John Blue Canyon road was too rough for anything but a beater sheepwagon, so years ago, the ranch had built tiny shacks and cabins, most barely big enough for bed and stove, on each of the separate ranges. The herders stayed in these while they tended their sheep in the lush feed and tedious close quarters of Little Mountain where the bands mixed easily. But when I arrived, it was summer. All the bands had gone up to the top of the Big Horns, leaving Doug to tend the bucks below on Little Mountain until they could join the ewes in the fall for breeding. The country was peppered with empty cabins, any one of which could have housed my childhood dreams.

Doug was small and gray, with the twinkly blue eyes of a leprechaun and his jeans held up by rainbow suspenders. "Well, now, I can hardly keep myself busy," he said in answer to my question. "But, you know, I bet you could set up camp in the Cow Creek cabin. There's lots to see up here. I could give you a horse. Strawberry'd be plumb fine for you. I've got about two of everything, salt and pepper, groceries aplenty. And a rifle. You'd need a rifle. Ever shot one?" By the time we'd returned with the sodas, our plans were made. When my sister and her husband left the next day, I wouldn't be going with them.

For the rest of that summer, I lived in the Cow Creek cabin, ten-by-twelve feet with a bed, table, wood cookstove and creek water to drink. Most afternoons, Doug would check in on me. He'd draw crude maps on scrap paper, showing trails, a homestead cabin, an old still site. Next morning, I'd saddle up Strawberry, a sixteen-hand red roan gelding, filling the saddlebags with lunch and a book, one map or another folded in my pocket. I hunted arrowheads out on the Honeymoon cabin point, scouted out the Bischoff cow camp on the edge of Cottonwood Canyon and explored dark, secret trails that lead down into the depths of Devil's Canyon.

On weekends, Miles would bounce up the seventeen miles of deeply rutted roads in his old Land Rover with wine, books, stories, an iced-down Sara Lee cheesecake. On one occasion, he arrived with Sonia, the new Big Horn County librarian, and her two children, recently migrated out from Lexington, Kentucky. She'd unfolded from the Land Rover, a lanky, dark-headed Dane with uncontrollably curly hair and crinkly eyes. "I've found you a fellow Kentuckian," Miles said, and our friendship was immediate, enduring long after my brassy romance with the paleontologist was over.

At summer's end, Doug rolled a Bull Durham cigarette in the crease of his jeans and encouraged me to return. "I'm sure we could get you a job lambing in the winter," he'd said. "You've only seen a tiny piece of this whole outfit. It's big. I can talk to John and get you a job."

I laughed at the prospect, sure of a more traditional future and certain it wouldn't be in the lambing sheds of Wyoming. But fall was hard. I was at a loss as to how to live my life and where to dig in. I saw people with companions, homes, meaningful work, but I had no idea how to become them, how to spin that web of comfort and belonging around me. I felt alone, unmoored and unworthy.

I'd been drawn to the racetrack, to the fog-wisped early mornings of Kentucky, the thin-skinned electricity of the thoroughbreds, the weathered coarseness and nomadic air of the track crew. I hot-walked and galloped horses in the mornings and loaded UPS trucks from a warehouse in the afternoons, living once again in my parents' house. One day, as I stepped from the shower, my mother saw the bruises that covered my body from handling truckloads of packages, and, trembling with frustration, she said, "You don't have to do this. You're smart and pretty and have an education. If you aren't doing exactly what you want to be doing when you turn fifty, it's your own damned fault."

I can see her standing there in the dimly lit hallway by the bathroom, next to the antique oak washstand my father had refinished. She was in her midfifties then, the mother of five mostly grown children and the wife of a minister turned president of a theological seminary. She hadn't yet gone back for her master's degree, which she got at the age of sixty and began her internationally significant career in the work of Alzheimer's care. She was a woman between lives and angry with her daughter for squandering the freedom and opportunity she must have envied.

I stood before her, bruised and lost, a young woman meant to be a success in something but not. Unable to distinguish words of love from banishment or childhood dreams from a place to hide, I packed my things and headed back west.

I'd gone because I was drawn to this nomadic life of horses and sheep and dogs. I'd gone because I was young and lost and had no idea where else to go. I arrived in the snows of February, twenty degrees below zero, and made my home in a sheep-wagon parked under the bare-branched cottonwoods of the Whistle Creek Ranch.

For fifteen dollars a day plus groceries, I pulled on coveralls slick with lanolin and paint smears and worked twelve-hour shifts in the long, low-slung Whistle Creek lambing sheds, where five thousand ewes gave birth in six weeks' time. At six in the morning, when the night-drop man went off shift and the day crew came on, the tiny wooden jugs that lined the perimeter of the shed would be filled with ewes and lambs brought in during the night. The jugs were small pens, roughly three feet by four, just big enough for a ewe and one or two lambs. In the midst of crowded corrals, ewes would sometimes birth their lambs at a high trot and never look back. Or, they could get distracted before they bonded, learned the smell of each other, and the lamb had a chance to nurse. Those tiny wooden jugs promoted love between mother and child, a forced closeness until the real thing took over.

It was my job every morning to brand the new pairings with numbered paint brands, one to a thousand in rounds of green, blue, black, red, orange. I'd check to see if each lamb had sucked. If not, the tiny space of the jug made it easy to drop into a squat and wedge the ewe against the boards with a shoulder while guiding the lamb's mouth to the teat and shooting a taste of milk through its lips. The ewes gave off the acrid smell of dank wool. The lambs had loose wrinkly skin and long tails. From down within the jug, the world would go silent as the lamb began to suck and the ewe would remember some-thing old and innate and give up her mad bleating in my ear.

When the lambs had suckled, the pairs—which sometimes included twin lambs—would be turned out into slightly larger pens holding four pairs, then eight. When the relationships passed muster, they'd get sorted outside the lambing shed into pens of twenty, then a hundred, moving in orderly fashion toward the bands of roughly a thousand pairs that would sum-mer together on the high reaches of the Big Horns.

In my first season, my sheepwagon was parked under the cot-tonwoods behind the Whistle Creek tenant house, along with five others parked in a row for hired hands and herders. The wagons were set so their Dutch doors opened to the east, to the morning sun and acres of hayfields that stretched out toward the sagebrush hills. At the far end of the wagons was an out-house, ancient and foul.

As the spring nights warmed, I slept with the Dutch doors open to the night and to the sounds of coyotes and owls. One night I woke to find the wagon lurching with the stumbling weight of someone coming through the door and across the tiny floor. It was Antone, the Basque night-drop man, and then he was at my bed, his tongue in my face, his weight on top of me with his stale sheep smell, his words slurred and stinking of alcohol. From within the protection of my sleeping bag, I yelled and knuckled his head and bit at his lips until he spit on me and finally left, cursing and muttering that he hadn't meant any harm.

It was my first experience with what alcohol could do to a

person. Among the herders, I would see it again and again. Someone fastidiously proud of his cooking or leatherwork one day could be barking like a dog or peeing in his pants the next.

I learned to be disappointed, my head down and my coveralls zipped around me. I began fastening the hook on my door and thinking of the hills and longing for the quiet, empty space of them.

## COON CREEK CAMP

From beneath a clump of sage outside the sheepwagon door, Lady watches, a short-haired heeler dog, red and speckled and slimmer than most. Her liquid eyes watch me now and claim me as her own. Every morning in the hour before daylight I have cooked for her magnificent, pleading feasts on the wood-stove: bacon carved from the slab, eggs scrambled with chunks of Velveeta, Bisquick hotcakes with syrup, all served into a pie tin at the edge of camp, beyond the lantern's light.

I'd come to the ranch wanting to herd sheep, a band of my own out in the hills in all the space and silence, an odd woman's vision of romantic life. I'd made it clear what I wanted, but John just said, "We'll see." And when the spring bands were made up and branded, disappearing into the greening hills with their herders, I was left behind to farm.

Days later, Sterling appeared at the edge of my field, arms flapping nervously to flag me down from the tractor. "If you still want to herd, pack your wagon and I'll pick you up in an hour," he blurted unceremoniously. "Larson's sick, and I've brought him to town." The old herder's mind had come unraveled, and when Sterling appeared in the morning to tend his camp, he'd found him muttering loosely to the sky.

"She can herd them all by herself," he'd said of Lady when he hauled me out from the ranch to these broken sagebrush hills where a thousand ewes and lambs had scattered for days on their own. But when he deposited me and my camp alongside Coon Creek and hauled the other wagon away, the herder's little red dog followed it almost to the highway, then fell back to the ridge above camp to howl long, thin notes for her lost friend, her one and only. My outstretched hands only pushed her deeper into the sage, so when I rode out on Willy at a nervous trot, she didn't follow.

Instead, I had Mike, a bully of a blue heeler that one of the farmers had given to me. Mike was tough and dense but hardly worth his dog food as a herder. He followed devotedly at my horse's heels, head to the ground and stuck like a tick to the thud of hooves, as though this were the safest place on earth. Bred to work sheep and cattle, he had spent his days instead growling at strangers from the back of a pickup. Faced with his ancestral calling, he wanted nothing to do with it, and like some sullen teenager, his eyes refused to meet mine, as if to say, *This ain't my problem.*

I had imagined making a big circle at an easy trot, giving loud whoops that would send the dogs racing and the sheep raining down off the ridges. I had imagined them collected and bleating in a tidy pool of wool alongside my camp below. But there was no above and no below, only mile after mile of crumpled, broken country with gullies and ridges splayed in all directions and sheep in twos and threes flung like pale rocks across it all.

I rode and rode as Sterling told me to do. In a late afternoon turning to evening, I rode as far as I could see sheep and kept riding because there was no end to the sheep until it was dark, and then I gave up.

The clouds that gathered low across the badlands all that afternoon had bunched against the mountains, erasing the eastern horizon and making the darkness total. My throat was raw from yelling at sheep who wouldn't move, and Willy's sideways prance had long since turned deliberate. So we moved slowly and silently through the darkness, his hooves knocking loose the bitter smell of sage as we headed home. It was several hours before I knew for sure that we were lost and that what pulled at Willy and made his step sure wasn't the sheep camp with its barrel of oats but his home ranch at Whistle Creek, eight or ten miles to the east of us.

I slept that night between saddle blankets, my face weighted into the fleece lining of my saddle, turned on its side and curved pulpitlike over my head. Around my palm I'd wrapped Willy's reins to hold him through the night, his muzzle dropped to my shoulder with what seemed to be resignation, maybe disgust. The dog I'd smitten with curses all through the afternoon and evening was curled into the hollow behind my knees, and I was grateful beyond words for that.

Through the frame of Willy's legs, I could see lights along the highway, miles distant, curving in the great silent arc of night. I imagined that each one was coming in search of me and watched for it to slow and waver from its path. None did, and I knew there was no reason that anyone would until morning. I thought of lovers long asleep in their beds. I thought about rattlesnakes. I thought of my family eighteen hundred miles away and wished that they knew to worry for me. I thought of Lady howling her sorrow into the night sky on the ridge above camp and thought her brave, or at least true, and envied her for knowing so surely what it is that she loves.


During the night, a light rain fell, little more than a mist that settled on the blankets. I woke often, without moving or disturbing the shape of us, to listen to the sound of our breathing, and when first light appeared, we were up and gone, easily finding our bearings and the two-track road that led us back to camp.

Sterling was waiting for me as I rode into camp, moving toward us with his brittle, choppy gait as though his feet never quite knew where they would find the ground. A foolish grin was spread across his face as he said, "Well, kid, thought I'd catch you in bed, but looks like you've already been hard at it."

When I confessed I was only coming home from yesterday's ride, I hoped for some sign of sympathy, but all he said was, "Don't worry, kid, I won't tell a soul."

As his offering to our calamity, he fashioned for me a "canned dog" out of aluminum cans strung together loosely along a stiff wire and fastened into a circle like a tambourine. With words that smelled faintly of morning beer, he instructed me to shake it at the sheep while hanging on to my horse. Handing it over, he wished me luck and headed back to town in his rattletrap pickup.

We watched him go until his dust had settled on the far ridge, the tips of Lady's ears visible above the sage, following the sound of his leaving. I was tired and discouraged and wanted to go home but too proud to say so. And there was no one left to say it to. I imagined for a moment climbing back up in the saddle and heading for the highway a free woman in search of a real job, then considered Lady alone in the sage and couldn't.

Instead, I began to cook. In a camp smelling of spilled kerosene and desolation, I began to cook for us all in the middle of miles of nothing. As if a full belly could make us powerful and a full plate could bring Lady over to us. Scraping at the pans on the stove, I noticed her ears had moved around through the sage to where she could see me work. She disappeared as I tiptoed a plate of meat and grease out into the brush for her but licked it clean when my back was turned. I courted her wholeheartedly with every trick up my sleeve, from Vienna sausages to Oreo cookies, and when I woke yesterday morning, I found her curled up in the dirt at the wagon door, her big eyes watching me without fear.

## McCULLOUGH PEAKS

Morning. Streams of pale light spill across the ridges like paint tipped over and flush from the sage the cries of small birds. From a ragged spine of rock, my knot of a thousand sheep begins to loosen as, one by one, the ewes and lambs trickle off the edges in search of fresh feed. The air is awake, alive with movement. It's May, spring in northern Wyoming, and I'm camped on the high benches of the McCullough Peaks.

At the edge of camp, Lady and Louise sit on their haunches and lean out into the morning with a working dog's earnest air of responsibility. Louise is a blue merle Aussie shepherd, a pup who has followed at Lady's heels and taken to the sheep in my second season of herding. She has one blue eye that speaks of righteousness. Today it says, *Sheep are leaving the bedground and your horse isn't saddled. We're ready. Send us.* Their faces turn in quick attention from sheep to Willy to me, coffee still in hand.

Picketed in a small clearing off from camp, Willy stands with his nose shoved deep into his bucket of oats. I gather my saddle up from underneath the sheepwagon and pack it to him, heaving it onto his back with a grunt. *In my next life I'll be tall,* I think, pulling the cinch up loose under his belly. Abruptly, his head swings up through the air, startled at some intrusion into the landscape. He stands frozen, watching so intently that for a moment he forgets to chew.

It's the horses that he sees. They slip down along the rim of the narrow canyon that falls from the peaks, widening and softening to spill into green feed below our camp. It's the bay stallion's band, one of three feral herds that range in the McCullough Peaks and whose paths we cross from time to time, sharing, as we do, the neighborhood.

They step lightly down the rim, coming closer to our camp and the sheep now streaming off the hill. There are seven mares, mostly bays and sorrels, two spring colts and the stallion, traveling off to the side but clearly in their lead. Among them, there is not one animal I'd call beautiful. They are small and dense and rough, the shape of their bones buried under coats still ragged with winter. Like the gnarled firs leaning from the winds at timberline, these horses are carved by the elements in which they live, not by any breeder's idea of perfection.

Still, you should see them move. All grace and ease, they move with full attention, like dancers seasoned side by side, their noses weaving the air to catch our scent. Together, their tough bodies express a single elegance, their effort one chord of survival.

I have watched them bear a storm. With butts turned windward and heads hung low, they shift their warm weight into one another and stand through whatever the skies pour down on them. From the comfort of my sheepwagon stove, I've felt my pity grow to envy of their loyalty, of their dependence on each other, of the sureness it allows them in a landscape that offers so little shelter.

This morning they stop just above camp, not fifty yards from us, at the edge of the hungry wave of bleating sheep. The stallion stands with his head high, studying Willy. The mares have an air both wary and curious, almost playful. One colt minces forward to sniff a woolly fleece, then leaps back from the surprise of it, stirring the mares into a ripple of snorts and skittering bucks. The stallion ducks his head, too, then shakes it in our direction like a dare. Unbearably tempted, Willy charges the end of his picket chain with a squeal.

A year ago they had taken him, calling him away with whatever power their freedom holds. On a wild, blustery morning with winds gusting against the flimsy tin of my sheepwagon roof, I had woken to see him, white eyed and snorting, straining against the picket line snaked in a tangle through the brush, and followed his eyes to the low hills above camp. Three wild bands had gathered in the coming storm to show out for one another, to strut in the electrical currents of air sweeping in from the north. The stallions had bunched their mares into three tight knots that circled and swung, finally slowing into a still point with only the wind howling and the stallions themselves moving between.

From a quarter mile away, Willy was charged by the tension and wanted to be gone into the middle of it. I did, too, so I'd been careful as I saddled him and pulled the bridle over his halter. I led him away from camp to climb on, but he reared and ducked his head, and the loose sheepherder bridle slid from his head to the ground. For a moment he stood between two worlds, his eyes to the hills, one ear twitching slightly to the rattle of the oat bucket and the grain sifting through my fingers.

I crooned to him. I groveled. You can have all the oats, anything you want. But his head swung around high to the horses on the hill, and knowing he was loose he moved away from us with the stiff-legged staccato movements of exhilaration. Then he was gone, bucking, twisting, stirrups flapping like wings, into the hills. The bands began to shift in the distance, the stallions confused by his presence, circling around their mares, the bands circling around each other, and all disappearing from my view in a roiling wave.

I remember standing for a long time watching the empty hills with the reins in my hand, the bit in the dirt at my feet, awed that my life could change so suddenly. There was no phone to call for help, no neighbor to flag down. Only a spidery track of dusty road whose miles would soon be impassable with the storm. I remember looking at my dogs and wondering if it were possible for them, too, to be drawn away from me by some experience more primally *dog*. I thought not, and wondered at the difference in Willy that took him away.

That year I celebrated my twenty-fourth birthday on foot in the rain, tearing a soggy tuna fish sandwich into pieces for Lady and Louise. For six days it had rained, and on the seventh, John chugged into camp at dawn, his truck chained up on all four tires to get through the mud, worried about what he might find when he got there. Willy had been found out by the highway, lonesome and cut up and looking for oats. As a gelding, he'd had no place with the wild horses and had been fought out of the bands by the stallions. Having gotten the news through the back-range grapevine, John showed up at first light with a spare horse loaded in the stock rack of his pickup and an aging birthday cake decorated with plastic flowers on the front seat beside him.

Now, a year later, if Willy has memories of the beating he'd suffered, they are paled by the sparks and snorts flying across the distance this morning. Heads are up, eyes are bright. In an air charged with invitation, I hang my weight into his head to draw him down, my own memories all too present.

I turn to the horses up the hill, their spirits like bright lights beckoning, and realize that I, too, want to be gone away. More than the caution of my isolation and more than the wisdom of my losses, I want to shake my head back at them. I want to *dare*.

I fasten the bridle over his head and pull the cinch tight around his belly. Cheeking his head around to me, I dance his dance, one foot in the stirrup and one foot touching the ground, until I pull myself into the saddle. *Do we dare?* In a sideways prance we step gingerly into the sage, and the horses' heads fly high, their ragged manes catching the wind.

How can we *not* run on a spring morning with our hearts

stretched wide? And so I lean only slightly, shifting my weight to give him his head, and we're both gone now, hard and fast and wild through the sage, the horses already bolted and bucking up the hill. One hand a clutch of mane and reins, the other anchored to the horn, I pledge myself on for the ride, the dogs yipping madly through the brush behind us.

Below us the ground falls away unevenly and leaves us stumbling through the air over sage and rock and the holes of prairie dogs. I lose my sight to wind and tears and close my body around the center of what there is to trust and trust it.

For long moments we ride their wake of dust and drumming hooves, suspended in a balance of fear and grace as hooves meet earth and the earth holds us up, following until our lungs and hearts can stand no more. Glittering and heaving, we fall to a stop and watch them take the ridge. They snort and jump and stamp their feet at us, disappearing over the top with necks snaking and heads shaking in triumph.

Turning back, the morning is spread before us, raw and brilliant, tumbling for miles into the desert basin below. The sheep are fanned in a great pale arc through the sage, and the birds cry out their morning songs. With corks popped off our sedated hearts, we turn down from the slope, changed, and pick our trail back to camp and the quiet rituals of our day.

# TRAILING

When summer heat comes to the basin, birds sing early and go quiet under a leaf of shade. Spring grass crisps beneath the midday sun, and the sheep go thick and logy in the still air. The pond below camp warms and shrinks, leaving behind a shelf of mud pocked with sheep tracks, urine, and flies, but since it's the only water for miles we use it. When the sun settles high and unforgiving, I send the dogs off to circle the lead, crying, "Way round, way round" into the dry air, and the far sheep turn back to camp, nearly running, their heads low, to sip at the fouled water and clump around its edges. Here they suffer the day, their heads tucked into the scant shade of one another's bellies, until the slanting light releases them back into the hills in search of grass.

In these early nights of June, the moon shines full, and the sheep travel through it, restless for green feed, a luminous, drifting mass that spills in rivulets through gullies and rises up hillsides, conforming intricately to the imperfect shape of earth. Their bleating is incessant. With muzzles blistered by the day's sun, they inch across the sparse range and, between clumps of grass, break into a brief and urgent trot, never lifting their noses from the ground.

My dreams are edged with the sound of their wandering. I wake each morning brittle and ragged with their longing, worried about where the night might have taken them. But out in this vast country, there is no place where I cannot find them, no lush farm field for them to invade, no neighboring band of sheep with which to mix. My early mornings are spent slowly arcing around them, tucking in the edges and counting the markers I can identify—the black sheep, the mottled, the disfigured—to raise the odds that I've found them all.

When the sun rises high and we're pinned beneath it, I turn binoculars across the basin to the Big Horns some sixty miles to the east, seven thousand feet above us, and watch the snow line retreating to the highest peaks. Sterling has shown me where we're going, pointing a shaky finger north to where the horizon bumps down to the lower bench above the Yellowtail Reservoir and the town of Lovell. "Little Mountain," he says. "That's where you're headed with these sheep next, but you can't start yet."

Every day I watch this hem of snow lift away from the bare

rock face in the shimmering distance, trying to imagine snow-banks melting into freshet streams and warming to the first blush of green mountain grass.

He kills the engine as his trail of dust catches up, billowing a fine sift of grit across us.

"God almighty, it's hot." Sterling lifts his hat and wipes his forehead with a shirt sleeve. He's traded his sweat-stained silver belly Stetson for a new straw hat that appears almost comical on this pinched and dour man.

"Yes and I hope you've come to get me out of this godforsaken place."

He sighs and pulls out a Camel. "Sorry, kid, but you're the last to go up. Lucka the draw."

He has told me this before, but in the heat I'm whiny and impatient. I watch him navigate the match to his cigarette, his fingers long and surprisingly delicate for a man who pushes at the hard edges of working and drinking. He keeps them moving so the wobble doesn't show, but I know it's there and know that when he leaves my camp, he'll go sit in the Medicine Wheel Bar on Lovell's Main Street. He'll drink whiskey ditches in the air-conditioned dimness and tell stories about me—not mean, not unkind, but with the proprietary ownership of the captor.

When the dust has settled, he shoves the pickup door open, gets out, and goes around to retrieve a Styrofoam cooler from the passenger-side floor, setting it down in front of me in the dirt. The cooler is brand-new and bright white.

"What's this?" I ask and lift the lid. Inside are two pints of strawberries, a six-pack of Coors, a package of frozen hamburger from the ranch locker, and a block of ice. I press my palms to the frozen meat and ice until they hurt, then raise them to my face and cover my eyes with the cold. When I drop my hands, the dogs are staring hard, their heads cocked in puzzlement.

"Won't last long in this heat, but it'll float your boat for a while." Sterling tries hard not to smile, but he's clearly pleased with his gift. I've never seen him flat out smile, much less laugh. The lines of his face are sharp and thin, pinched around the mouth. Maybe his mouth no longer opens wide enough to smile, or maybe he's just so long out of practice.

"Thank you, Sterling. Nothing's tasted good, hot as it's been."

"The ol' lady'll prob'ly scream to high heaven when she sees fresh strawberries on your grocery ticket. But hell, I couldn't pass 'em up. She drives her damn fancy car, and you can at least have strawberries." Then he adds, "I remember how it is." He's snuffling around the pickup, pulling more groceries and mail out from the clutter piled on his truck seat.

"Thank you, Sterling," I say, my hands still lingering in the cooler.

"And that six pack ain't from the outfit. I bought it for you, myself." He stares hard for a moment at the shimmer of mountains in the heat, his jaw set against the pleasure of this last gift.

In all the weeks that he's tended my camp, Sterling has seen to it that I've had the necessities. Early on, he'd measured my head with a string and on the next trip brought me a silver belly Stetson. "That ball cap don't cut it in the sun all day," he'd said. "Got to carry your shade with you, 'cause you sure as hell won't find any out here." And then, "Looks good, kid."

The following week he brought a Winchester .30-30 lever-action rifle and five boxes of shells. "For the coyotes and for anybody else out here that don't belong. You know how to shoot?"

"Yes, I shot a twenty-two on my grandfather's farm growing up." Which had some little truth to it. I didn't want him leaning over my shoulder to show me how.

It all got charged to my ranch account and taken out of my three-hundred-dollar-a month paycheck, but all the same they'd seemed like gifts.

Sterling pulls a small calendar from his shirt pocket and runs a finger over the page, studying it.

"So when do we go up?" I can't help but ask.

"Friday. Friday, I'll move you on over to Larry's Last Pond. You'll just have to stay put there till we can get everybody else goin'. Then I'll move you over to Dead Horse Pond, where you're on deck to go." He emphasizes this last part as though we're rodeo ropers about to bust out of the starting box, but in fact we are a slow, tired, hot, and cranky bunch looking to get out of here.

"Once we get everbody else up, I'll come back and start you. It'll be about the middle a the month."

"Who was Larry, anyway?"

"What?"

"Larry's Last Pond . . ."

"Oh, hell, I dunno. Some old guy out in the middle a nowhere, I guess. I'll see you Thursday mornin' about nine, and you can take the ranch truck in and do your woman business. Don't drink all that beer in one splash, now."

"I won't, Sterling." Though I can't for the life of me imagine why it would matter.

Sweltering hot. Sterling came today to stay with my sheep while I went to town to get a filling from the dentist. He sent me off in the ranch pickup with words of caution: "Be careful, and don't forget to come back. Make sure'n get all your woman things you'll need for the summer."

It felt good to drive. I shopped Main Street in less than an hour and bought all kinds of things I needed for the mountain—new saddlebags, boots, warm gloves, socks, underwear. And I treated myself to a long, silky nightgown and a soft pink corduroy robe. I'd thought it would seem like a homecoming, with familiar faces crowding the street, but anyone I knew was off on a tractor or out in the hills. I came back to camp as soon as I could.

The real gift was this morning, early, in the first gray light when I trotted off through the sagebrush to get around my sheep before Sterling showed up. Though I wasn't even looking, a pale chiseled spear point caught my eye. Right there on top of the ground.

Before first light I called up the dogs and took out horseback for the rock ridge where the sheep had bedded the night. It was move day and we started early because of the heat. While Ster-

ling hooked the pickup to the wagon tongue, I held the flashlight and listened bleary-eyed to my instructions.

"Well, kid, these old gals know where they're goin', so you
just have to stay behind 'em and keep the little'ns bumped up.
But if it gets too hot, they'll plum bog down and you'll be dark-
thirty gettin' to camp. Short trail, this'n, and an early start. You
should make camp by ten or eleven."

The sheep trailed easily through the early light, eager to be
going somewhere and knowing they were heading to the
mountain. A half mile out from the new camp, the lead ewes
smelled water and began running toward the pond, leaving
their lambs to straggle behind. I gave one last push, then cut
around, letting the bunch sort itself out, and headed up the hill
where Sterling was setting up my camp.

From a distance, I could see that something was wrong. He
was moving in and out of the wagon with a choppy thin-legged
gate. Tarps were scattered all over the ground, cardboard boxes
of groceries tipped on their sides. As I rode closer, he began to
include me in his stream of conversation, though he wouldn't
look at me.

"Nearly lost the whole outfit on that washed-out sum-
bitchin' road, and I got no idea how this miserable outfit
expects me to pull a goddamn thing in this sorry, weeny-assed
pickup. Jesus H. Christ."

Smoke was coming out of the chimney. He'd started a fire in
the wagon's woodstove, and through the open door I could see
my new coffeepot on top of the stove. But in the sage outside
there was a glint of shiny metal, and looking closer, I saw its
aluminum basket and percolator stem stomped flat in the dirt.

As I dropped from my horse, he slowed his tirade and

looked sheepishly around him, realizing I'd caught him in his tantrum. Following my eyes to the ground, he said, "Got rid of them goddamn coffee guts for you, kid. A waste of time if ever I saw one."

During lambing, Sterling ran what was called the outlaw shed. To this small, low shed, attached by a fenced alleyway to the main shed, were brought all the unpaired and unloved: ewes whose lambs had died, lambs whose mothers wouldn't claim them or had no milk, the smallest and weakest triplet born to a single ewe. The orphaned lambs were bottle-fed until a ewe who'd lost her own lamb was brought in. Sterling would neatly skin the dead lamb, rub the skin in its mother's afterbirth, if he had it, and place the "jacket" on one of the bums, lacing it together at the throat and belly with a few stitches of baling twine. Sometimes the ewe took to her new lamb with enthusiasm, or maybe required coaxing and even baling-twine hobbles around her hind feet so she couldn't kick the lamb as it tried to nurse. But once the orphan lamb was filled with the ewe's milk, her smell would begin to seep through its pores.

Somehow Sterling found the patience to stitch the little jackets on the gangly lambs and trick the pair into a bond, but his infamous temper made him an odd choice for the job. Just a few years later, he would shoot himself in the head with a pistol in one of the cheap Lovell motel rooms frequented by herders on a binge. But in these months, he coaxed the new relations until he could remove half-rotten jackets from potbellied lambs and worry the devoted pairs into an outside pen to join all the others.

On this oilfield road, there is traffic. Trucks come and go, not a lot of them, but more than nothing, which is what I've seen all spring. The pumps are scattered through the hills and from a distance look like fat hens pecking their heads to the ground and up, to the ground and up. No big lights or platforms. Men drive this road to check the pumps, check pressure gauges and I don't know what else. Their windows are rolled up against the heat and dust, but they look hard trying to figure me out, and then they wave. Sometimes they stop.

This one man who stops tells me he does leatherwork, that it's how he passes time in the motel room until he can go home to his family. When he asks what size belt I wear, I'm wary and say, "I don't know. I don't wear a belt." Then he asks if he can measure my waist and make me one, and I don't know why but I say yes. He seems sincere, and I'm lonesome. He's soft faced, his pale skin burned bright. He smells clean. He unhooks his belt and pulls it out from the loops of his jeans. He tells me to hold up my arms and kneels down on one knee and wraps the belt around my waist. I can see his scalp because he's taken off his ball cap, and he's so close I can feel the heat rising off his body. I think that maybe I shouldn't be letting him do this, but what comes to mind is my mother fitting me for a school dress, not some scared feeling, so I let him. He pulls a pencil from his shirt pocket and makes a mark on the back side of the leather where it meets the buckle. "There," he says, and stands back up. "Give me a couple of days."

I let my breath out and watch him climb back into his

pickup and drive away, not knowing at all whether I have the whole world spread around me, the luckiest woman, or if I'm a prisoner in my own special jail.

In this desert country, water is hard won. On average, five to seven inches of precipitation fall on low-elevation ground that grows what can survive it. Sagebrush, four-wing saltbush, greasewood, saltsage, spare clumps of slender wheatgrass, Indian ricegrass with its panicles sprung open like fireworks. After a spring rain, tiny pricks of grass emerge from spidery cracks in shallow hoofprints, a fringe of green appears around the edges of rocks where moisture has some slim reason to collect. Narrow gullies conceal streamers of color twisting and turning beneath the surface: white and pink phlox, copper mallow, mariposa lilies, yellow mustards, tender patches of pale wild violets. Only the evening primrose, *Oenothera caespitosa,* blooms exposed on the brittle hardpan. At dawn their ivory petals haven't yet contracted to reveal the pale pink underside but are still spread wide open like transparent moons fallen from the sky during the night.

The heat is oppressive with no breath of air, no shade for miles. I splurge on rationed water and fill a bucket and stand naked on the cottonwood stump at the wagon door. I tilt my head back and pour it all on my face and down through my hair, spilling over my back and down to the ground. For just this minute I'm cool as my skin prickles and the sunlight sucks the moisture from it. Below my feet the cottonwood takes on the smell of wet river-bottom shade and shelter, the water disappearing into the dust.

Antelope nibble on sage leaves, waiting delicately for the storm. I've been watching it simmer in the western sky, steely gray closing in over Heart Mountain and swallowing the northern Absarokas. The air is still, the sheep stunned quiet by the heat. Then there's a puff of breath from the east, and another, the feel that something's happening. This must be what war is like, nights spent quietly waiting for bombs to release this tension in the air. To the west, jagged silver branches dart through the charcoal sky, the thunder indicating that the storm is ten or eleven miles away. I can hear, before I feel it, the wind shifting from east to out of the west, and it sounds like a convoy of semis in the distance. I watch it whip and tear dust from the ridge road, coming toward us. I want to be anywhere but here and imagine a plush hotel room with drawn curtains, running water, and movies on television, and maybe popcorn, too.

On the knoll above Larry's Last Pond, my sheepwagon's metal chimney is the highest thing around. Sterling has said I'm safe with the metal tongue propped up on a block of pine. Lightning will hit the chimney, he tells me, come down through the stove and the metal frame of the wagon, then get grounded by the rubber tires and block of wood. But the stove's only four feet away, and the block of pine's maybe a foot and a half tall and slim comfort against it all.

I move Willy's picket down off the crest of the hill and pour a measure of grain onto the ground for him, wishing I could bring him inside. The sheep are loud with complaint now and moving off the water and out into the hills, away, as if there is shelter within reach. Would some other herder go after them, I wonder? I call the dogs into the wagon and feed them each a big finger of peanut butter from the jar. We sit with the top door open and watch the storm come.

When it hits us, the temperature plummets and sheets of rain and hail blast the wagon. I latch the door shut and retreat to the bed, as far from the iron woodstove as I can get, and call the dogs up beside me to wait it out. Lightning explodes around us, thunder in deafening cracks and menacing growls. The dogs pull up closer as the wagon rocks and tilts in the wind. I hold them close and sing to them, to me, a lullaby, "Sweet Baby James," because it comes to mind. Within moments, the gullies are running water, and beads of hail pelt the wagon. The sheep are running, too, the few I can see through the window above my bed. The wagon smells of kerosene, peanut butter and rank dogs as lightning flashes and thunder rumbles our insides.

This storm's moving fast, and when it passes, I saddle up and slog through the mud to look for sheep and bring them home. The sun comes out strong, and the hills glitter with pockets of hail, streams of water. There are puddles in every nook and cranny, three ponds that had been bone-dry now filled. We quietly move up the west ridge, Willy intent on his footing. From the cliff, I can see the sheep below and one dead ewe, struck by lightning. Out of this silence I give a whoop to turn back the lead sheep, and from below the cliff, a golden eagle lifts from its hidden perch, its wings a good six feet across and beating the air with a *whap-whap-whap* right before our noses. Willy shies and stumbles over his own feet, sliding nearly to his knees in the mud and catching his balance as the dark figure rises up and is gone away from us.

Home late, I fix the dogs a skillet of eggs and bacon and gravy and bread and give Willy an extra scoop of oats. I'm tired and ready for bed, grateful to be alive. Tomorrow morning, if Sterling can get through the mud, he'll move us on to Dead Horse Pond.

"Not sure I'm cut out for this package," Sterling grumbles. He's got his pickup all chained up to get through the mud, and he's crabby. His body gives off the sour smell of days and nights spent drinking. "Was gonna leave you a day to dry up, but that greasy bastard Rudy'd be cryin' to get up the mountain. Jesus, I'm done when I get these pansies up top. Give the whole bunch back over to John and good riddance."

Then, as though remembering I'm there, he asks, "How'd you make out in that storm?"

It's on the tip of my tongue to say I'd never been so scared, to ask if herders get killed by lightning. But I can tell he's not really listening, not interested in anyone else's drama. "Fine," I say. "No problem."

"Tuesday we'll have everybody up the mountain, and I'll come start you up on Wednesday. Five days' trail from out here, so eat your Wheaties."

I watch him fight my oat barrel up into the pickup bed. "Do you need some help?"

"Hell no, not that it'd matter if I did, half-pint that you are. Get on out there. You're on your own now till Wednesday, and I'll be here at dark o'clock, so be ready. And don't let them oil-field guys give you any grief. I seen their tracks all over."

I leave him to his black mutterings and climb up on Willy,

heavy in my muddy boots. The dogs are at our heels, and I call them up to the sheep, "Way 'round, way 'round. Push 'em up, push 'em up!" They sweep the bedground, nosing up stragglers, and the old ewes come running back for the lambs. The damp air is full of sage and wet earth and the bird sounds of early morning.

Miles drove over from Little Mountain in the Land Rover around noon, bringing Bennie Ruth and Freya along. They're getting ready to open Natural Trap Cave for a season of archaeological work, with students coming in from around the country to work three-week shifts at the dig site. Freya is Canadian, living in Lovell, and will handle the cooking there. Miles and Bennie Ruth are from Missouri, both PhDs. He teaches paleontology at the university, and she, psychology at a private women's college. They have what, in the seventies, was called an "open marriage," opened in the past somewhat bumpily to include me.

When they arrive, it's like having a circus come to town. They have news of the world beyond the ranch, of politics and music and the crew gathering for the summer's dig. They're smart and funny and excited about their lives. I let my sheep scatter as we drink beer, eat cheesecake and watermelon under a sky that again has turned clear and blistering. Now my camp feels like the center of the universe, all that I need. They give me a whole box of cassettes, from Jerry Jeff Walker to Chopin, and wave and honk as they pull out. "See you on the mountain!"

When they leave, everything feels barren and empty, no

longer nearly enough. They consider me brave and said so, thinking that this is some hero's world I'm living in, a child in nature and all that, but they don't know the rough edges. They see only what I choose to show them.

I open the leftover Sara Lee and pull a finger through the cherries and the sweet cream cheese, then saddle Willy and begin the long, slow circle around the sheep, bumping the strays back toward the center. Horseback again, my world begins to fall back into place around me—sheep, dogs, and a horizon that I know intimately. I'm relieved, once again, to have my bearings.

Sheep gathered and bedded, I drink a last beer and dance with the dogs out under the stars to the Rockport Blues Festival and African drumming, my last night before we begin heading to the mountain.

The days are long and the country desolate. We trail from before five in the morning until almost nine at night, with a few hours' break midday when the sheep clump around the water hole and pant, too hot to move. Little Mountain looms larger with each mile, and looking through binoculars, I imagine that I can see the cabins above me. Sand Draw camp the first night and Little Sheep Mountain the next.

From there, the sheep leave before dawn and hit the trail on their own. They know where they're going and have an urgency about them, like when they're thirsty and smell water. I leave camp and pick up stragglers, bumping them up to catch the lead. We make it to the highway by seven thirty and to the canal to water by ten. Since we're so close to Lovell, Sterling lets me take the truck into town at noon, and he stays on the water with the sheep. I let myself in to Freya's apartment to borrow her shower, my first in months, and use every sweet-smelling thing she has. I buy chocolate milkshakes at the drive-in, one for me and one for Sterling. Tomorrow we'll cross the Yellowtail Reservoir on the causeway bridge and camp that night at the base of the mountain. Looking through my binoculars now, what I thought were cabins are only snowbanks.

John Hopkin meets us coming into Roundup Springs that evening; he's taking over tending my camp for the rest of the summer.

"In the morning, you'll need to bump up the tail end and get 'em moving pretty good with your dogs; then they'll just have to drift up that slide-rock trail by theirselves." He points to the bright scar of braided trails on the mountain face. I notice the fine red hair and freckles covering his forearms and the chunky gold ring on his right hand. "It's too steep for you and your horse, so you'll have to work your way up there a bit to the north. Pick your way careful and watch your horse. You're better off leading him if you think you can hike it. Some of these old guys can't, but hellsakes, what good's youth and beauty if you can't climb a little rock?"

John is all arms and legs and whistling energy, clad in mysteriously clean jeans and a polyester shirt with ironed-in creases. In charge of all the sheep and herders, he works like a fiend from sunup to sundown and yet here he is with his pickup washed and waxed and a cloud of aftershave in his wake. After a spring full of Sterling's dour spirits, he's a breath of fresh air, and it occurs to me there might be more on top of this mountain than just green grass.

"I'm gonna pull your wagon on up around to the big mountain where you'll have it for the summer, but you'll have to stay in a junker for a couple weeks in the meantime. Anyways, pack up what you'll need till you get up to the forest permit. And leave your fine china behind. This John Blue Canyon road's a son-of-a-gun and it'll bust cast iron to pieces. And where you're goin' you won't be needin' your damn prom dresses, either." When he chuckles, he tilts his head back slightly and his face crinkles, all sunburn and freckles.

It's dusky evening and the sheep are still drifting up toward the vertical slide-rock trail that we'll climb tomorrow morning. The mountain face looms over us, we're so close, and its bare rock echoes back the chaos of sheep bleating for their lambs behind them and for the green grass above them. It makes me nervous, but John says they know where they're going and some will begin pushing up in the night. He said, "Quit your worrying; you're just about to start your summer vacation."

"Well, hell, looks like you made it." John has been waiting on top of Little Mountain with a cold Coke for me and a barrel of spring water for my dogs and horse. "I tried to getcha a room at the Holiday Inn, but it was plumb full up," he says with mock earnestness when he sees me wrinkling my nose at the old dark sheepwagon he'd hauled up for me. The sheep spread through the thick grass, eating their fill, beaching in clumps all around us with the sun hanging high at noon. "Rest a day now, and we'll trail you one more jump on up Mexican Hill and over to your camp on the rim of Devil's Canyon. It'll be your last camp before we take you on past the Medicine Wheel and up to your forest permit at Burnt Mountain."

When he's gone, I wander back over to the rim to look at where we've just been. The trail had been a bear, climbing between cliffs and around tilting slabs of slide rock—easy for sheep and rigorous, if not dangerous, for a hiker, but for a horse with slippery iron shoes, nearly impassable. We'd made it, though not without false starts and backtracks to find the single spot of grace that might let us through.

From this elevation gain of nearly three thousand feet, I can see the shape of the Big Horn Basin and all the miles we've covered. Through binoculars, I scan the long, dark face of the Absarokas to the west and past them into the deep heart of the Yellowstone backcountry. I follow the Absaroka Range north to the Beartooths, where they disappear into Montana, and then east to where the northern Big Horns and Pryor Mountains reach toward them, nearly closing the circle. Out in the center of the basin, I pick out the knob of Heart Mountain and spine of McCullough Peaks, sixty miles to the west of where I stand. And to think that we've walked and ridden across the whole of it all.

I call Lady and Louise over, and we fall down into the grass to nap with my jacket bunched up for a pillow and the sun warm on my face. We are tired, all of us. The grass around the wagon is sprinkled with spring beauties and shooting stars, lush enough to rise up around us like nests where we're sprawled, dead to the world.

## BURNT MOUNTAIN

In the summer of 1978, when my mother was grieving her sick and aging parents, my father bundled her into the car and drove her west across the Great Plains to a log cabin in the northern Big Horns, off the Sheep Mountain road, tucked in among lodgepole pine and Douglas fir.

The cabin belonged to the Lewis Ranch and was where John stayed while tending the summer bands on the national forest permits. He met my parents there among the profusion of wildflowers the mountain gives up that time of year, loaded their bags into his four-wheel-drive pickup—its stock rack freshly painted red—and brought them as gently as possible over the rough miles to my high camp on the top of Burnt Mountain.

My mother seemed a young girl when she arrived, as though she'd shed some thick skin of habit as she was brought across the country to a place she'd never been. When my parents emerged from John's pickup, they were both bright eyed and silly with the extravagant remoteness of where they'd landed. "We've had such a trip!" she exclaimed, then told stories of cooking meals en route on the car's manifold, an idea she'd read about in a magazine. My father laughed, relieved by my mother's lightheartedness. As I welcomed them with hugs, their bodies felt thinner than I remembered, unprotected by the humid Kentucky air and the rituals of their lives. At ten thousand feet, the air was cool and startling in its brilliance, shimmering as a thing in itself that had shape and color. He pulled a sweater around her shoulders as she said, fiercely, "This is *beautiful.*"

I tried to see anew what they were seeing for the first time. There was the sheepwagon, a gypsy camp on wheels, with its rounded metal roof and smoke coming out of its chimney. The lower body of the wagon was wood, rough and splintered, painted what was once a jaunty red. Across the back, above the window, HOME ON THE RANGE was lettered in crude brushstrokes. The wagon faced east for the morning sun, and from inside its split Dutch doors, there came the small rhythmic explosions of coffee perking on the woodstove. The rubber tires were snugged into holes in the ground to level the wagon and anchor it into the hillside for when the winds blew up hard.

I remember wanting all this to be a charming picture for

my parents to see but thinking how it might seem slim comfort against a yawning emptiness that stretched a hundred miles up into Montana. And how, when you're used to sheltering hardwoods and rolling hills, the bare-bones immensity of Wyoming can make you feel like a sacrifice left on a slab for the gods to pick clean.

John began unloading supplies and boxes of groceries from the back of the pickup, and we pitched in. A hundred-pound sack of oats for Willy. Dog food and a pair of rawhide hobbles that I'd asked for. The usual groceries that came every week, mostly in cans: soup, stewed tomatoes, tuna fish, beans and corn, and cling peaches in light syrup.

Spotting the Spam and Vienna sausages hidden underneath, I fall into my weekly ritual. "John, you know I hate this stuff. I'm feeding it to the dogs as soon as you leave."

He smiles sweetly at my parents, unloading their bags, and tells me over his shoulder, "You'll find your sorry ass planted in four feet of snow one morning and you'll be damned glad to have this shit in your cupboards, pardon my French." He resumes his whistling and empties the oats into the galvanized metal can by the wagon.

My parents' eyes are twinkling as they carry their things over, unused to this blasphemous variety of affection. I take their bags, marveling that they've packed so lightly, and lead them up into the tiny sheepwagon that will be their home for the next few days. My mother first, then my father, stepping up onto the block of pine and squeezing past the kitchen cupboard on the left and the woodstove on the right. The interior space is small, the floor only three feet by four and flanked on both sides by a bench with storage bins underneath. With three of us inside, there's hardly room to turn around. My mother runs her hand over the quilt on the bed, a gift from a family friend, with diamond-shaped ripples of color; then she reaches up to finger the wildflowers that I've gathered into a mayonnaise jar on the bookshelf. "What are they?" she asks, and I name them, separating the tender blossoms of each as I do so. Silver lupine, sticky geranium, heartleaf arnica, yellow monkeyflower, shooting star, bistort, wild blue forget-me-nots. My father leans over my shoulder, watching, his breath warm at my ear. I speak the Latin names, too, because I know them and because my parents are still listening. *Lupinus argenteus, Mimulus guttatus, Eritrichium . . .*

They have driven eighteen hundred miles to be in this place where I am. Now they're here, and it is all so close—the scent of soap on my mother, the rare, bright fragrance of flowers, the roof of the sheepwagon curving over us, barely clearing the tops of our heads.

She appears at the wagon door dressed in faded bib overalls that are rolled up at the ankles. Underneath, a waffle-weave thermal top and a denim workshirt, bleached out like the overalls to the softest shade of blue. On her feet, coarse work socks with brown reinforced heels that spill over the sides of her gardening tennis shoes. She shoves her hands deep in the pockets that hang low on her hips and smiles winningly at both Dad and me, knowing we must be shocked.

I've never seen my mother in blue jeans before, much less baggy overalls. She steps down onto the woodblock step, and I come up close to look at her. "I've been going through Daddy's things," she says, "and I just wanted to bring these along." She is a handsome woman, square jawed and bright eyed, slender and strong. Now she looks like some fierce Huck Finn, her face wavering between joy and despair, full of her daring. She shakes her hips, making fun of herself, but it is her father's life that she wears.

I reach up to touch the fabric at her waist. It smells of fresh laundering, but underneath, inside the weave, there's the smell of hard well water and blackberry-bramble sweat and the dark, sweet lingering of Burley tobacco leaves curing in the fall air. My mother had grown up working alongside her father in his tobacco fields, trying to match his stride and energy and dawn-to-dark ambition. She had hoed her rows the fastest, milked her morning cows first, and graduated valedictorian of her class for the chance to have the bright light of his approval shine on her. Now he sits in a wheelchair, in a nursing home in the small Kentucky town where he used to buy his tractor parts, clouded in the confusion of Alzheimer's. For my mother, there have been years of caring for him, of trips to the farm and a live-in companion, but finally there is nothing that's enough and no place where he feels at home. She stands on the wood block telling some story about her father over my head, to Dad, to the sheep creeping over the rise of the hill. Looking up into her animated face, I can see that she doesn't know how to mourn his loss. I have no words to comfort her; instead, I lift a hand and help her down.

The top of Burnt Mountain is above timberline. To the south, the bald ridge runs fat and smooth like the back of an elephant out to where it rounds into a grassy knob. From there, you can see where Half-Ounce Creek springs up and quickly drains into the headwaters of the Little Big Horn River. To the north, the ridge climbs and narrows into a spine of fractured shale where the sheep are now gathering, dropping to their knees, panting with the great weight of their fleeces, to bed down for the night. Their bleating quiets as lambs suckle and butt at their mothers' bags.

My parents have unpacked their things into the sheep-wagon cupboards, and I've pitched a small canvas pup tent for myself off to the side. We have eaten mutton stew around the small table in the wagon, and now the sweet and vast spaces of evening have drawn us back out.

It is the last magic hour of light. A red-tailed hawk screeches. The dogs lie out among the clumps of Idaho fescue, heads stretched down onto their paws, done for the day. Below camp, the Burnt Mountain spring falls through a tangle of wild sweet arnica into a catch-pond, the mud around its edges stamped by sharp hooves, its glassy surface filled with a day going to dusk.

I lift my binoculars and follow the slope of grass, gone velvet and rich in the last light, down to where it tilts into timber half a mile below our camp. I look for straggling sheep, for coyotes with their coats backlit like halos, for elk nosing out to feed, then scan the skewed horizon to the north where the Leakey and Dry Fork ridges reach out toward the Little Big Horn canyon, one from each side, like arms grasping for what has already disappeared. I watch for movement and pass the binoculars on to my parents.

When I begin to pull fat chunks of split pine from the woodpile, my father steps over to help. He has buttoned his heavy wool shirt against the chill and looks more rugged than the man I grew up with.

Every Sunday until I was eighteen, I sat in our family's pew while he conducted the service in his black robes and spoke the words of Christ and the teachings of the great theologians. His voice was deep, his diction perfect. From a distance, I watched him speak and move through a world that was polished silver chalice, crimson velvet stole. His words were of love and truth, carefully chosen, and he spoke bravely, a habit that could make the righteous uncomfortable, and on occasion, there were threatening phone calls in the night. I heard members of the congregation say they couldn't have made it through the hard times—unplanned births, sudden deaths, rebellious teens, alcoholic spouses, the grittiness of life that tests people's faith—without my father. I heard them say, "You must feel so lucky to have him as your father." Now here he is beside me, gathering up an armload of wood with his fine hands like an artist's, one knee bent into the soft dirt. Chips of bark sift down into the creases of his jeans. His breath is raspy, labored with the altitude. Up close, he seems like a man I do not know.

We carry the wood back to the fire ring and arrange it loosely in the bottom. "No kindling?" he asks. I shake my head and reach for the can of diesel fuel by the wagon steps. "John calls this my fifty-cent fire," I say, pouring it over the pile and striking a match, the flames leaping up in a whoosh of sparks.

My mother has rolled stumps of unsplit pine closer to the fire for us to sit on. Settling down on his, my father leans forward to say, "We were back in Nashville last month for a lecture at the church, and everyone asked about you. They all asked." His eyes are kind. His face breaks into a million tiny lines as he smiles, just like mine does. He laughs and says, "We couldn't help noticing that as a minister, I'm the shepherd of my flock, and now you're the shepherd of your own. Like father, like daughter."

"More like the black sheep," I say with a laugh but mean it.

I'm squirming with all the attention, foolish with my delight, and wondering just when it was that I began to take my leave. My mother once told my brother that of her five children, I was the one she could never hold, that early on I'd always break the embrace and toddle across the floor away from her. Born the fourth of five children and sandwiched between two sprawling boys, I later chose the ease of retreating over the bruises of competition, to be the silent one and learn to succeed by keeping out of the way. My leaving took me to empty back rooms with a book, to tall orchard grasses by the creek. If these places were lonesome, they were also magical and private. I learned to entertain myself for hours with fantasies in which I was the hero, the special one, the one who could ride the horse that no one else could ride. When I was older and had a horse of my own, I packed a book and a sandwich and left on free days to roam the hills just outside of town. Then after college, I found this ranch that would feed me and pay me three hundred dollars a month to ride, read and tend to the sheep.

Wyoming was my childhood's private world blown larger than life, with a horse, two dogs, a rifle, a wilderness. For this lonesome child, it was the perfect landscape, where isolation was sharp but safe. I had discovered a place where no one expected me to do or be much of anything. My fellow coworkers were tender alcoholics, muttering derelicts, societal rejects, and I had found a certain delicious comfort in their company.

The diesel has burned off, and when the flames take hold of the wood, they put out a sharp heat that sears my knees. *Black sheep. The wayward one, the odd one, the uncomfortable one.* The sky drops into darkness and the world becomes small, the shape of firelight on our faces. My mother's is wistful, expectant, my father's, bemused and content. I lean into the fire, rocking nervously on the uneven ground. I know how to be the forgotten child but not the only child, the blessed one.

Agnus Dei. Take away what I cannot bear.

"We just like to say that we raised a free spirit," my mother says.

Night. I lie in my sleeping bag in the old tent that smells of the ranch's musty basement, my head protruding slightly from underneath the flaps. What I see is stars, a far-flung glittering of icy space that I search intently for what I know. Cassiopeia, the queen, sitting on her throne, and Cygnus the Swan, the Northern Cross flying above her, and the slender arm of the Little Dipper reaching out of the northern sky to fill its cup. The night is almost silent. There is a ewe bleating on the ridge and the fire crackling close by in the sheepwagon stove. I hear the muffled voices of my parents, settling into bed. Then quiet.

My hand slips beneath the band of long underwear and rests on the smooth skin of my belly. There is life there, but I can't imagine it, only want it to be gone. In ten days' time, after my parents have left, there will be snow on the ground and more falling from the sky, the wagon door open and the spattering snow hissing on the hot iron stove. I'll put a few things—clean jeans, a T-shirt, my toothbrush, and a book—into a clean plastic garbage sack, fold it over, and slip it into a burlap sheep-salt bag, with a slit cut through the top to make handles.

My sheepherder neighbor, Grady, will appear on horseback to see me off. I'll leave the sheep in his care, slip the coarsely woven sack over the saddle horn, and, with a gloved hand, wipe the snow off the seat. He'll squeeze my hand and say, in his soft Alabama drawl, "Now don't forget to come back," and I'll ride down off the backside of Burnt Mountain, into the dark timber, toward John's cabin, a thin music sifting through the branches of evergreens. Feeling oddly content to be so bundled up and moving through the weather, I will find myself singing through the trees as well. Leaving horse and dogs at the cabin, I'll drive four hundred miles up into Montana to see a doctor and turn around and drive back the next day, emptied. Tonight I can't imagine how it will be, just want it all to be over.

A coyote yips. I lift an ear from the rustling of the bag to listen. From the ridge where the sheep are bedded, there comes an answer, one howl, then a chorus rising up. My rifle's in the sheepwagon, but I don't want to disturb my parents. I've never tried to shoot a coyote anyway, wouldn't want to even if my aim were true enough. If I were in bed tonight with the Winchester hanging below the bookcase, I'd fire a shot or two through the open door, straight up into the stars. I might yell something, just to hear my voice. *Eat mice, you lazy bums!* Other nights when maybe the day has been too quiet, I might clear my throat and let loose a high-pitched keen, part howl, part prayer, wavering up into the sky. Lady and Louise would be at my feet, heads cocked and eyes dark with indignation at my behavior; then they'd take quick, furtive glances out into the black night. Silence. Maybe a sheep bleating far off or the crickets' soft drone. If I'm lucky, they will answer. One yip, maybe from a young one who doesn't know, then perhaps the whole bunch will join in for the sheer joy of it.

Either way, it's just our nightly conversation.


Around the lip of the pond and sprawling down into the swale below the wagon, the sheep lay panting, knit together by the heat of the midday sun. Along the edges, some ewes have already heaved up onto their feet and begun feeding, heads down and tearing at the flowers in tiny jerking motions. "Hey girls, hey girls," I call Lady and Louise up from beneath the wagon and send them on to the sheep. "Push 'em up!" All at once, a thousand mouths open into a frantic, bug-eyed bleating for mother or lamb, a roar of longing. The dogs swing back and forth behind the sheep, sneaking in to nip a heel when the coast is clear and holding their ground when a mother turns to stamp her foot and glare. The ewes squat spraddle-legged and pee before moving out, the smell sharp and sour in the heat.

"This is the easiest sheepherding allotment on the mountain," I tell my father, who's mounted on the buckskin gelding John had brought me as an extra horse. Wearing a ball cap low over his eyes, he kicks the horse into a walk with the heels of his hiking boots. He's never ridden horses much but sits his saddle easily. I point to the rocky ridge behind us where my mother is bent over the fractured pieces of shale looking for fossils in what once was the ocean floor. "That's the highest point on my range," I nearly shout over the din of the sheep. "And sheep always go up. If I turn them loose from any place on this allotment, they'll end up there by dark."

The sheep are moving now, like some great ship getting under sail, and we follow along behind letting the dogs do most of the work. We're headed off the top, pushing the sheep down over the edge toward the thin timber that rises up out of the Little Big Horn meadows. My father, reins in one hand and cap in the other, is swinging and slapping his thighs, calling out to the sheep with abandon.

"Hey, hey, hoooh!" His face is browned and relaxed. His boots beat a soft rhythm on the buckskin's flanks, but the old horse pays no attention, moving always at the pace he chooses. Watching my father, I begin to understand what I couldn't have imagined—that he's having fun in this end-of-the-earth place I've claimed as my home.

I'd seen it in my mother the day before when she and I rode down off the top to go fishing with Grady. Dad had gotten a ride with Jack, the government trapper, to buy a fishing license at Bear Lodge. But Grady had promised to take the two of us fishing the "sheepherder way," which, being illegal, required no license. He led us to a tiny snowmelt stream that fed into the Little Big Horn, one that we could straddle, a foot on either bank, in most places. He untied a small hand net from his saddle and, whispering in his Alabama drawl, showed us how to hold it underwater with one hand and spook the fish into it with the other, then handed the net to my mother. After many, many tries, barefoot with her father's bib overalls rolled up to her knees, she scooped the net into the air with a wild shriek of excitement to find that she'd caught a tiny brook trout. Her face was that of a child, open wide in wonder at the surprise of the rosy fish flipping in her hand and the cold water streaming over her bare feet.

We had eaten trout for dinner, three brookies scooped up with the net and another that Dad caught in the late afternoon with his fishing rod before hiking back to camp from the river bottom. We sprinkled them with pepper and salt and cornmeal and fried them up in bacon fat in the iron skillet.

Now I watch Dad work the far edges of the sheep, tucking in the stragglers with a veteran's proficiency. Whooping and hollering, arms flapping and body swinging in loose-jointed motion, he has disappeared into a world of his own, as though the roar of a thousand sheep has rendered him invisible. Now I understand that he, too, longs to break the rules, to be the child who explodes in joy.

The ground drops off sharply below us into fingers of lodgepole pine and Engelmann spruce that reach up along the sides of Burnt Mountain. We give the sheep one last push down into the thin stringer meadows; then I wave my arms to Dad to just let them go. We turn our backs on the whole mess of lost ewes and lambs, bleating like stocktraders on Wall Street, and head back up the hill. "They'll sort themselves out," I say to his questioning look. "When the feed's good and there aren't any other sheep around to mix with, the best thing to do is just trail them down to fresh feed and leave them alone instead of fooling with them."

Dad nods his head in understanding or maybe just to the

beat of his gelding's newfound exuberance as we head back toward camp and the possibility of oats. We have plans, later, to ride over to the snowbank on the north side of Rooster Hill and bring back salt sacks full of snow to make ice cream with the grouse whortleberries we've picked. Our plans for the afternoon are comfortable ones.

I remember everything about their coming and nothing about their leaving. In my memory, they simply disappeared. John must have come and picked them up. There must've been hugs, good-byes, promises to gather as always for Thanksgiving or Christmas. I don't remember. What I suspect is that I was the one who disappeared first.

If my parents had been able to ask why this remote mountaintop seemed a safe haven, I couldn't have answered with any other story than that of the heroine, the adventurer, the brave one. We didn't have the language of failure to describe the dark howl that simmered below the surface; our only words were those of success. *What do you love? What have you lost?* If I could have asked both these questions of my mother or father, what would I have been able to hear? We did what we could. We spoke the words that we knew. I gave the names of the rough beauty in which I hid.

My father had brought my mother eighteen hundred miles to see me. As a young woman, I struggled to be enough for them, to pass muster in what I thought was an inspection. But he brought her to me in her grieving, and many years later, I am profoundly touched by the simple faith of his gesture. He brought the woman he loved across the whole country. Yes, to fresh air and open space, but also to me—for solace.

That we loved each other is clear. That we fumbled in that love is painful. What we had, in our shared blood, was the grace to lay ourselves out under a vast and forgiving sky and let its steady winds blow over us.

# HIDDEN

---

Outside, bears roam the dark and lodgepole pines give in the wind, their tall, thin spikes waving against the stars. Elk appear, ghostlike, their noses testing the night air for scent, and silently fill the open meadows to graze. Two horses stand side by side, and three dogs watch the night for what we cannot hear. Below us all, the Little Big Horn River falls into the canyon and runs to Montana, leaving behind only the sound of itself rising back up the valley.

In a battered aluminum kettle on the stove, he heats water, lots of it, and closes the wagon door and window tight against the chill night air. The space inside becomes thick with heat and moisture and pitch pine snapping and popping and water rumbling toward a boil, water dripping down the bulging sides of the pot to explode and hiss on the cast-iron stove. From the cupboard under the bed, he pulls frayed towels and washcloths and puts them into the kettle, still folded, poking them under the water with a big wooden spoon. On top of the covers he arranges a rough canvas, folding it to half so that it neatly covers the bed. On top of this he lays a clean dry towel and then another, overlapping, together as long as a person's body. "Now it's time," he says to me. I heel my boots off, set them upright in the corner and tuck my socks inside, then skin my jeans to the floor and underwear, too, and fold them in a pile on the bench along with my shirt.

Bowing under the roof's curve, I crawl on the bed and roll carefully onto my back, straightening the towels beneath me as I watch him at the stove, maneuvering hot towels out of the pot with fencing pliers and a wooden spoon. He's short, compact, and wiry, his legs bowed slightly with the years and his silvered hair bright against skin that's nut-brown and weathered. He's still wearing jeans and cowboy boots but is down to a T-shirt in the heat of the fire. He holds each towel high, letting the water stream back into the pot—busy, preoccupied with the order of his project, like a mother fussing over a meal.

He'd been raised in Alabama and still had the deep, slow drawl of the south after all his years in the west. He'd ridden the rails after the war, hoboing, picking up jobs catch as catch can. When John had hired him onto the Lewis Ranch, he discovered that Grady had a knack with dogs, that under his care they learned to work precisely and eagerly and with great heart. He'd discovered, too, that Grady offered the same to him, away from the barstool and the booze, out in the hills where his soul was aired out and quiet.

Now he's dropping the towels into an empty pan at the side of the stove. With heavy leather gloves, he wrings the water from them and stacks the twisted lumps in a dishpan. "Okay," he says, and turns to me with a steaming towel. He loosens the twist and tests the heat with his cheek, then gently lays it over me from my neck down across my lower belly. The heat makes me cry out softly and then go quiet, stunned. He smooths the towel over me and presses his palms against the hollows and mounds of my body where hands fit easily. I close my eyes and feel the heat driven through me, almost more than I can bear but not. Another steaming towel, laid lengthwise and covering my legs, and I feel my body disappear completely under its weight. He brings a washcloth to my face and presses it across my eyes with both hands, and when I feel my face soften, he begins to wash it. Under the blanket of heat, I am still, and only my face tilts toward the touch. He moves across my forehead, wetting the hair away from my face, and cautiously into the corners of my eyes. His hands tremble slightly as he works and his head, too, side to side, palsied, a dry drunk. On his fingers I smell tobacco and garlic and kerosene as he wipes at the creases along my nose, my chapped lips, and the corners of my mouth. His hands cover my face, and my mind drifts, imagining the leaves of aspens shimmering, tender to the wind, against my skin. I hear his voice ask softly, and with some amusement, "Does this suit you, ma'am?" as though I'm some lady in a spa, and I open my eyes and smile a little in answer. He's smiling a little, too, and his gray eyes are clear, the skin around them creased and weathered. I cannot find in this face the man I've seen on the streets of Lovell and will again come fall, barking and staggering, with a husky whiskey laugh, a face bloated like a pumpkin, and his false teeth lost somewhere along the trail from bar to bar.

He turns to the stove and retrieves another towel, loosens the twist and layers it on top of those already draped across my body. He smooths the corners and goes to my feet with a fresh hot cloth and spreads my toes and begins to work between them and down along the soles of my feet as if this is all he was ever meant to do in the world.

In the yellow, uneven light flickering from the kerosene lamp, I can see the steam beaded on his forehead and smooth upper lip. I see his lips moving and know that he's whispering to himself, to me, as he works, but lost in the heat and the roar of fire, I cannot hear him.

There is only the sound of fire crackling and water boiling, and beneath the heavy towels, my shoulders have softened in the comfort of this odd tenderness. I feel alone but protected, a thought that lets me breathe deeply. The winds gust against the wagon and my eyes close to the heat, the care and the belief that in this dark place I am hidden, if precariously, from the world.

I see her walking the dirt road up Burnt Mountain even before the dogs, sprawled in the dirt asleep, thinking their work done for a time. From where the road comes out of the timber into the open grass, it's maybe a mile to my camp. From her husband's camp on the lower reaches of the mountain, at least another half.

Lila's alone, and with binoculars, I watch her walk slowly, her gaze to the ground, aimless in her route as though she's not intending to come here to this place but might only happen upon it. She stops from time to time to pick up some small object and turn it over in her hands. Rock chips, arrowheads, fossils, maybe flower blossoms. She's put in her time at sheep camp and knows how to make something out of nothing, to make empty time a full day. As she comes closer, I see that her pants are a pale color and cropped short, that she has on thin tennis shoes and a plaid sleeveless blouse in the heat. Closer still, her head lifts to study the wagon as she picks up her pace. I set the binoculars down, though I know she can't yet see me back in the shadows.

She'd come west from Massachusetts as a young woman to teach high school English in one of the small communities of the basin. One summer day she drove her visiting grandfather up into the Big Horns to see the high mountain country, and they came across a man by the side of the road with a horse, a dog, and a band of sheep. I can imagine their enchantment, the car slowing, the window rolling down to the fresh mountain air, the sound of sheep bleating and stock-bells tinkling. At some moment in the exchange of pleasantries and the request to take a photo she would have realized that she was in the presence of a man who could match her wit. She must've also imagined him matching her adventuresome spirit, and there would have been some invitation to follow up with another visit, perhaps a picnic. I can't know what followed, but I can picture the courtship, the family wedding back east and the bright adventure of heading out into the Wyoming hills as newlyweds with high hopes and their band of sheep.

The dogs are at the edge of camp now, leaning toward her, bristled, waiting to see if this is friend or foe. I look into the small mirror by the door and wipe at my face with my sleeve, peer unblinking into my eyes, and listen to my heart rattling loose in my chest. I turn and smooth the covers across the bed, close a drawer, come back to glance out the door, then arrange the stack of books on the counter, straightening the spines so she'll be able to see them, see that I'm smart, see that I'm a good person.

Pinned to the wall above the books are cards from friends and the calendar where I record the weather, the visitors and the dead. I'd begun with crude drawings of sun or rain or a stick figure ewe on her back with her legs splayed high in the air and a vulture circling overhead. As the days passed, these squares had become more elaborate and within months become a series of tiny watercolors, one inch square. I smooth the pages and level them behind the books. *This is all I am and nothing more.* I think of the herders in their perversions, their drunks, their strange ways and want to believe in this moment that I'm one of them, accountable only for my sheep. Nothing more.

With the sun high overhead, the wagon alone provides shade above timberline, so when she arrives, I invite her inside to the benches. "The boys are napping with their dad," she says in explanation. Her graying hair's cut short and is damp around her face, her breath labored with the altitude and the weight she carries, but she still has a clipped and feisty Massachusetts diction after all these years.

"I could heat the coffee?"

But she shakes her head, and I remember, embarrassed, that as a converted Mormon she wouldn't drink it.

"Water, then?"

"Yes, that would be wonderful."

Her face softens, and I lift two thick mugs from the hooks by the stove and carry them down to the spring box, dogs at my heels. I dip them into the icy water bubbling up from the ground and feel my fingers go numb. I'm thinking to chill the mugs themselves as a hospitable gesture, but with my back turned, I linger in the wavering reflections and the sense that my body could take root here and never move, the flies buzzing and water gurgling through invisible cracks in the earth. I feel the numbness creep up through my fingers and up my arms, pleasantly, solidly, until I know for sure I've been away too long.

She's waiting for me inside, leafing through the stack of books. I set the mugs down on the table between us and pull an open package of cookies from the cupboard. When I sit down, we are nearly knee to knee in this tiny space, and then there's nothing else to be done and nowhere else to look.

"So, how are you? What are the boys up to this summer?" My heart is pounding and I gather to myself images of the other herders at their worst, fouled and stumbling through their January binges, and I want instead to hiss, *This is all I am, and you can't expect me to be more. All I am. Nothing more. Don't ask.*

"They're good," she says. "Summer ball's nearly over and we start back to school in a couple weeks." Her voice is shaky, seemingly directed out the door. She pauses, considering whether to answer the first question. She turns to me and her mouth collapses into an uneven smile. "They miss their dad, but it won't be too long before he's down the mountain and out in the hills. Not so far from us then."

We both study the view, and the sheep beginning to peel off the pond below us, trickling out into their afternoon graze.

This woman who sits not three feet from me could tell me when it was that the small disappointments began to gain on the joy. She'd be able to say when she first saw the hole in her husband's soul open up and swallow him, leaving behind a stranger. But I don't risk this question, sure that I would be included in the tally of her losses.

Her sudden movement startles me back to the present, and when I turn, she's working to push herself out from behind the table. "I need to be getting back," she says but then lingers, flushed, and looks me in the eye, and I see there are tears in hers. Having made to leave, she does not.

"Are you all right?" My voice is sharp with concern, as though I didn't know all there was to say, but I say nothing. *I have chosen my safety, and you walking up the road, sitting across from me with eyes moist and full of a sorrow you will not name, you cannot uncover me.*

She shakes her head, almost imperceptibly, not so much no to the question as no to answering. "It's a long way back, and they'll wonder where I've gone." Still she doesn't move, as if she means to say more. I wish myself back at the spring, my hands in the icy water, longing for the cold to creep up through my limbs and clutch my heart. She shakes her head again, this time to clear her thoughts. "Thank you," she says, and finds a smile to take her leave. She steps heavily from the wagon to ground and begins her long walk home.

Maple stands at her picket below the pond, her head hung in a doze. An evening breeze stirs and lifts a thatch of flaxen mane, whispers her tail, then stills. She's a muddy sorrel, a caramel that deepens to black at her knees and hocks. Her head is all of one color, dished, with dark, wide-set eyes. Her mane and tail are light and shot through with hairs of black and brown, her near hind foot white.

John had brought her to me several months before, late in the spring. "I run the phony bastard off. Called hisself Buffalo Bill and fancied hisself a horseman, but he run her ragged. I got a little meat back on her bones and her sores healed up enough for saddle if you pad her good. But she could use a little TLC, if you know what I mean."

"What's her name?" I'd asked.

"Hellsakes, I don't know," he'd said, cocking his head and stooping down to tap the ash of his cigarette on a rock at his feet. "I bought her off the trader late in the winter and don't know that she's got one. Ol' numbnuts musta called her something, but for the life a me I can't think what."

When I lift the lid off the galvanized metal trash can that holds her oats, an ear twitches, and she lifts her head, watching. I scoop a Folgers can full and dump it into her pail and put the lid back and push it tight. Stepping up into the wagon, I find an apple in the sacks beneath the bench and pull the table out and slice it into a rough dice, scrape them off the board into the pail and mix them down into the grain until each bit of apple's stuck with oats. As I step down from the wagon, she nickers softly.

A moon has risen unnoticed in a sky not yet dark, a thin rice-paper moon that's almost full. I set the pail to ground and run my hands along the warm silk of her neck. "Hey, sweetheart, you got the big soft eyes today. You got the big soft eyes, yes you do." I unwrap the loosened latigo and let the cinch drop and pull the saddle and blankets from her back in one motion and rest the saddle on its horn and lay the blankets flat in the grass, bottoms up to air out even though this whole day we'd never ridden them to a sweat. The dogs move closer and then lie down, one head on the twist of stirrup leather, another on the pad, their eyes back and forth between her hind feet and me.

I sweep the brush across her round belly and the sores healed and grown back white haired at her withers and, lower down on her side, the half-moon shape of cinch ring. She raises her head high, bobbing it, sending grain and slobber falling from her mouth, and curls her upper lip in protest at the fruit. "I never met a horse that didn't know an apple." The dogs lift their heads at the sound of my voice. Maple steps one foot forward and lowers her head against her leg, rubbing it, and then goes back to her grain. When I run my hand down her near front leg and squeeze, she lifts her foot, and I move the flat side of my pocket blade around the inside of the iron to loosen the dry, caked mud and a stone, then check that the shoe's tight. She lifts each foot when I ask and have asked every day for the last month. When I come back around to the last, I see that she's cleaned the bucket, leaving only a few pieces of apple in the bottom. I scratch the hollow between her jaw bones and clean the crust from the corners of her eyes while she rubs her head against me. "Oh, you're sweet, oh you're good. You're my precious, yes you are." Across her back the sky has softened to periwinkle and violet, and against its darkening the moon becomes luminous, as if gathering to itself all the light being lost to us. I rest my cheek against her neck and watch the sky, daring to imagine the life now gone from my belly, and the tears I hadn't allowed myself leak down my cheeks.

I lean into her neck and spread my arms up around her, thinking she'll move away, but she shifts to me and I lean the whole of my weight against her and smell the warm salt of her skin and ride for a while the rise and fall of her breathing.

## MEDICINE WHEEL

The sheep move silently now without their lambs, knowing the trail and where it leads. Snow sifts down, thin, almost rain, a cloud disintegrating to ground, and the wind rattling through the trees confirms what the calendar page does not, that winter's coming and we must leave the mountain. We trail the dirt road along the Little Big Horn and turn through the timber into the broad flats past Rooster Hill and the low wooden corrals at the Sheep Mountain Road, where weeks before we'd trailed and worked the sheep. There we ran them through narrow alleys and cutting gates, separating lambs from ewes with semitrailers backed up to the loading chute, and we pushed the lambs up ramps, loading them carefully into the maze of compartments. As trucks pulled away, the ewes cried out in search of their lambs for a day, then two, and then afterward came an eerie silence as though something essential had been forgotten, lost.

Through the sleet, John's pickup appears with water and oat barrels tied into the stock rack and my sheepwagon hitched behind. "Have you got jacket enough? Want to get in and warm up, have some coffee? I've got my winter coat behind the seat here if you need it, but it'd come to your knees, not that you'd mind that today."

"I'm fine. Maybe some coffee." I sidle Maple over next to his window and lean across my saddle horn, letting the accumulated sleet drip off the brim of my hat.

He unscrews the cap off a Stanley steel thermos, pours a pale brown cupful, and hands it through the window. "I'm gonna get on up ahead of you on the road and wait at the cattle-guard past the Medicine Wheel. I'll get a good count on the old biddies comin' through the gate."

I peel off soggy Handy Andy gloves and hold the cup warm in my hands. "I wish you'd learn to make real coffee."

"Shit. Get yourself up to Bear Lodge then. If you trot on out, you might get there by dark."

"I'll suffer."

He lights a cigarette and rummages through a cardboard box on the passenger floorboard. "Here, you better take these." And he hands me a pair of new leather gloves with gray wool liners.

I trade the empty thermos cup for the gloves and shove my wet ones down into the saddlebags.

"And you may as well fill your pockets, too." He tears open a package of Fig Newtons and holds it out in the sleet until I manage to grab a handful with the too-big gloves.

"John?"

"Hmm?" He tilts his head out the window to look up under my hat and into my face, as if waiting to find, make, or do whatever it is that I need.

"This summer . . . I don't think I've ever quite said thank you for all you did." His gray eyes the color of thunderstorms, looking up at me, not blinking. "You know, the doctors and all."

He pulls his head back out of the sleet and takes a drag on his cigarette. "Oh, hell, that was nothing." He blows smoke away from me into the passenger side and then taps his ashes out the window. "I'm just glad you're okay." His eyebrows are knit together in a frown, but a shy smile creeps across his face before he looks away.

The skies have turned the color of raw wool and so thick that the lead ewes have disappeared into the fog with only the sound of their bells tinkling. Lady and Louise have ducked under the front bumper, trembling as they watch the sheep drift out of sight beyond their reach. I zip my collar up around my neck and fasten the top button of my slicker, the chill gone to my bones already with miles yet to cross. I raise a gloved hand into a reluctant farewell. "I'd better get."

"Okay, see you up top." John leans forward to start the engine but stops. "And just so you know, this is between you and me. Ain't nobody's business but ours, and you can take that to the bank."

· · ·

We push hard up the trail-riddled slopes that fall off into the headwaters of Porcupine Creek and down into Devil's Canyon, the dogs working them until the lead ewes find the narrow gravel road that climbs Medicine Mountain toward the radar station notched in a peak and the Medicine Wheel beyond, and the sheep begin to string out beyond my sight again into the frozen fog.

I drop from my horse and walk to warm my feet across fractured shale and fossils, the tiny alpine phlox of summer surviving still in cracks and crevices. With the altitude, the sleet has hardened to snow and lightened to something I can lift my face to. There is the soft rattling of sheep hooves clicking across stone, the tinkling of their bells, the thud of Maple's iron shoes following behind, and the *swish-swish* of the long yellow slicker against my jeans. The ground levels off in the cloud, and the sheep disappear into it along the two-track and shale, John waiting somewhere ahead to see them through the gate. I follow behind, picking up stragglers and walking with the dogs to the far edges to listen because we can't see much of anything.

Out of snow wisps appears the tall chain-link fence that circles the Medicine Wheel, its woven wire studded with remains of pilgrimages, and I veer from our path to follow its perimeter. Thin strips of cloth, once bright reds and yellows and greens, are now bleached by weather and silvered with the gathering snow, tied in ribbons and fluttering limply. The wires are full of gifts: prayer bundles of soft hide and cloth, small animal skulls, branches of sage, beads strung on rawhide thongs, a silk scarf wind whipped into soft fringes, an eagle feather, a small bell hanging silent. Inside the fence, rock spokes wheel out into a circle some eighty feet across and, within it, another, ten or fifteen feet wide. Around the far edges are six oval stone cairns, only a few feet long, now filled with offerings, but might once have held a person singing. All of this from some distant time that no one knows for certain, five or maybe eight hundred years ago, on this day receiving the first dusting of winter, soon to be covered in deep snow for months to come.

Without an offering myself, I look around for possibilities and end up pulling from my saddlebag a wet and frozen glove, traded earlier for dry, and work the fingers into the wire so that they're spread skyward. *For all I have.* I weave its mate next to it as best I can, though it looks more clownlike than I would have wished among all the hopes and miseries tied alongside.

I walk beyond the fence to the west edge of cliffs and look out into the cloud, into the miles of what I know is there, but I can see only the ground falling off to cliffs and crevices. What I know to be there is the whole of the basin, and to the far west, the Absarokas and the steaming sulfurs of Yellowstone. In this place where I stand fires were lit, signals sent and answered, and still now the Crow, Shoshone, Arapaho, Sioux, and Cheyenne gather to sing and pray here, so close to the sky.

The dogs sit their haunches, leaning out over the rocks below and the squeaking of marmots among them. When I reach for the saddle horn and pull myself horseback again, they turn and fall in at Maple's heels. We complete the circle, stepping carefully around the rock edges, and follow the sheep as the ground begins to tilt back down toward the sound of John's voice calling out to his dog and, beyond that, to the trails that will take us down.

# HIGHWAY

It is late April 1979, and thin puffs of clouds sail through the sky. Between them, a wash of sun warms the air where I sit, watching the empty highway below and scanning the horizon for a red Volkswagen beetle. Seeing nothing, I turn back to the rise of hills behind me, where my sheepwagon's parked, my horse picketed, and, hopefully, my dogs are curled up and staying put. I'd been stern with them, feigning a gruffness I didn't feel to make them stay. They'd been puzzled, cocking their heads to one side, whimpering. We don't go anywhere without one another, but this is different. This afternoon I'm headed to town.

My alarm clock's in my jacket pocket, and having checked it once and again, I know what it says: that it's past the time we were to meet, five thirty, and there's nothing to do but wait. If something's happened to her, I'd have no way of knowing. With the fuzzy fingers of my Handy Andy gloves, I work the dried mud and sheep manure from the creases of my boots and wait.

Last week, tending my camp, John had brought a note from Sonia and slapped it down on the sheepwagon table with a dramatic sigh. "Jesus. I told her I'm not supposed to know one damn thing about this, but if you're goin', just point your bunch towards that far knob there and they'll be parked sure as shit when you get back. Now don't make me come to town lookin' for you."

"What's going on?"

But he's already out the door and unloading a bag of horse feed from the back of the pickup. "Just read the damn note. I don't know a thing about it, and if you go off on a toot, then I won't be claimin' any part of it."

As a rule, the sheepherders that work for this outfit are pretty good, but even the best are strung tight. John's had his share of pulling herders out of the bars because some tourist dropped off a six pack of beer or a bottle of wine.

Sonia's note said that our friend Gretel would be giving a reading at the community college in Powell and that we were invited to have dinner beforehand with her, the dean, some professors, and the poet who was reading with her that night. If I gave John the okay, she'd pick me up at the highway and bring me back home afterward. *Please, please,* she'd added at the end.

"I told her it's a lucky thing, you bein' so close to the highway here. Otherways, once you got back in the Peaks, she'd never be able to find you in that little car." John's voice is soft, his actions meticulous. Having unloaded the oats and water and groceries, he's now sweeping bits of debris from the bed of his truck with a whisk broom.

"Tell her I'll be there. What time?"

"Five thirty, she says, at the highway turnoff. Now do you have anything to wear that don't smell like sheep shit?"

I spot her miles away. Hers is the only car on the road, and when she pulls into the gravel turnout, I'm standing there.

She honks the horn and, jumping out the door, gives me a hug. "I'm here to swoop you off to civilization—electric lights and flush toilets! A real kidnapping." Sonia's dressed in a bright full skirt, a linen jacket and a pale silk scarf wound around her neck. She's Danish, and her dark wispy hair is full of curls. She opens her arms to the hills and spins around. "What an address you have!"

She is the Big Horn County librarian and has, in the three years that I've been herding sheep, brought me the gift of books, many of them and wide ranging in topic. The library itself is in the town of Basin, but she makes monthly rounds to all the outpost branches in the county, some no more than a few square feet in a post office or community hall. She added me to her list early on, boxing up thirty and forty-pound collections of literature, biography, and a wild assortment of whatever intrigued her. I imagined her moving among the shelves like a sorceress adding treasures to a boiling pot—Mildred Walker's *Winter Wheat,* Cather's *Song of the Lark,* Stegner's *Angle of Repose,* a book on color and design, paintings of the French impressionists, edible plants of the Rockies, a brief history of China. "These are for your sheepwagon library. You can keep them as long as you want—no late fees." On occasion she'd add her own exotic surprise, whether a head of elephant garlic brought back from Laramie, a pair of lacy pink panties, a bar of chocolate, or a swath of fabric for a tablecloth or curtains. Always there would be a note, either a card or just a brief scribble on library stationery.

Her responsibilities took her the breadth of a county that was a hundred miles across with only one stop light anywhere. That was in Greybull, whose Main Street banners proclaimed it the HUB OF THE BIG HORN BASIN. With her car full of books, she'd crisscross the county to the libraries in Tensleep, Hyattville, Manderson, Greybull, Shell, Emblem, Otto, Lovell, Frannie, Deaver, Byron, and Cowley, infusing their collections with new titles and recycling old ones into fresh homes. In Cowley she would deposit my box of books at the Waterhole Bar, across the street from John's trailer, for him to pick up and haul out to camp.

Inside the car I suddenly feel shy and foolish, blushing under my sunburn and feeling a tomboy in her company. I hold my hands to my nose and smell the Jergens lotion I'd worked into my skin, but still there's woodsmoke and kerosene rising up out of my pores and out of my clothes. As she pulls the VW out onto the highway, I search the hillside for my dogs and feel I've left half of me behind.

"So, happy birthday. Forty, right?" My lips are chapped and the words come out squeaking.

"Lord, yes, can you believe it? And"—she pauses—"I have a story. I've been seeing someone recently, a man who has a place south of Shell on Trapper Creek. Such an interesting man, works for the railroad, a naturalist, and has a beautiful log cabin along the creek."

She goes on to tell me he'd invited her for a birthday dinner at his home over the weekend. She'd offered to bring something, a salad or bottle of wine, but he'd said no; just come. So she drove the eleven miles to Greybull and the twenty to Shell and turned north on Trapper Creek Road. She wondered what he might cook but didn't know him well enough yet to know. Still a bachelor—maybe steak on the grill or a jar of Ragú heated and poured over spaghetti. Any of it sounded like an adventure, and she was glad to have someone to celebrate with.

When she turned onto the gravel drive that wound down toward the cabin, she saw him sitting on the wide steps of the front porch, plucking a pheasant he said he'd just run over with his truck driving home.

"Happy birthday, and welcome to Trapper Creek," he said. "Dinner will be just a bit."

"Roadkill for your fortieth. Could be quite a year ahead."

"But the wine was fabulous," she tells me, smiling.

Sonia holds herself carefully, nearly Victorian in bearing, but has a wide open, racy streak that in those early years surprised me. The divorced mother of two daughters, she'd moved them here from Kentucky and taken this job, arriving a year ahead of me. We discovered soon after meeting that our paths had already crossed. She had taught school in the Nashville grade school I'd attended, then had gotten her master's in Lexington about the time I would've been there on summer breaks from college. Miles, the paleontologist from Little Mountain, had introduced us in the summer of 1976, knowing that we shared a connection of place, but what he couldn't have known then was that these were just two of a generous handful of seeds that would germinate and start up the trellis, sending out runners and binding us together. We don't know this yet, but in the years to come, we will marry, divorce, trail cattle, throw baby showers, celebrate birthdays, build campfires, mourn losses, and weep together. We will follow each other, without question, through all of the changes that life brings.


When we arrive at the Lamplighter Inn, Gretel and the poet haven't yet arrived. But there are ice cubes in the water glasses and hot water in the bathroom sink and—yes!—toilets that flush. Sonia musters up diversionary small talk while wine is poured and I sit wondering about my dogs and horse, picketed at camp, and watch the doorway for our friend.

I'd met Gretel a couple of years earlier in the Lovell lambing sheds when I'd driven in from Whistle Creek for supplies. She'd come to Wyoming to make a film about sheepherders and stayed on. We'd become friends because we both loved dogs and horses and because women were scarce at sheep camp. My first summer herding on the forest permit, she'd spent much of it living out of the headquarters cabin with John. She'd brought a big editing machine and was finishing up her film, tending camps with John and helping when she could, and I'd see her once every few weeks. Or John would bring messages: "Grets is comin' your way tomorrow. Says she'll ride over, so leave about eight if you want to meet her halfway." From my high camp on Burnt Mountain, the trip was only about three miles down the backside of the mountain, around Rooster Hill, and across the big flat meadows along the Sheep Mountain Road. She would arrive bearing gifts in her saddlebags, a bottle of wine or maybe T-bones plundered from the ranch freezer, local gossip and stories from the part of her life I didn't know—New York, California, some ranch in New Mexico, someone's play being produced in London.

Sometimes she disappeared back into her other world, and John would show up at my camp with a report: "I don't know where the hell she's gone this time. She put on her fancy pants and packed up half her shit, but she left the goddamn movie machine in the spare room, so I know she'll be back." And he would smile, his auburn freckled face crinkling into tiny lines, and laugh softly, hardly more than a sigh. No one I've ever known could cuss like him and make it sound so much like tenderness.

Salads come and then prime rib, rare, but still no Gretel, no poet. The dean disappears to make phone calls; watches are discreetly checked. "Well," he said, "there must have been some mistake, though I'm sure we'll meet them over at the hall."

When they come tumbling into the lecture hall, we discover that we'd been sitting in different parts of the same restaurant, the two of them in the café with the cheap menu and the rest of us in the formal dining room with amber shaded lights and crushed velvet drapes.

"We thought we'd been fired," Gretel roared hilariously. "We had to buy our own goddamn dinner!" And then, to me, "Does John know you're playing hooky?"

A crowd has gathered, and it's time to begin, so Sonia and I take our seats.

When Gretel reads, she becomes someone I'd never seen before. I knew that she'd danced and was making documentaries, but had no idea she'd written poems. She gathers herself up with a dancer's grace and speaks with sureness and care.

> Probably she is a river where
> seasonal mixtures run
> rich: watercress, hot springs, ice floes stacked
> in clerical collars on robes of
> dark water folding and
> unfolding around her.

Her voice is cadenced, heavy. *Snowdrift, comet tail, wounded deer,* the words that come out of her are surprises. Gone is the toe scuffing and the flippant cowboy humor, the scattered profanity that I'd come to accept in her. That was all wind in the trees and trash blowing around, and what we glimpse this night is the wind itself, powerful and clear. Sonia's knee nudges mine, and we look wide-eyed at each other in surprise.

What had seemed obvious in the light of day is less so in the narrow beam of headlights, but there it finally is, the red bandanna tied to the wire of the highway fence where my dirt road splintered off from the highway.

"Will you be able to see? Can you find your way back?" Sonia worries as we slow down and stop.

"Of course. It's not far." I dig into jacket pockets for my gloves and feel my alarm clock, bulky and out of place. The sun of the afternoon, the anticipation and the waiting all seem a world away. I'm sleepy, dead tired, and ready to be back in my bed, to bring my camp back to life. To make my world whole again, all that I need.

"I could drive you up the road."

"No, it's far too rough. I'm fine, really."

She keeps the headlights on the gate as I crawl through the wires, and then I wave good-bye into the glare and watch the headlights retreat and swing away from me, illuminating a wide swath of sage and fence, then blacktop. I zip my jacket tight and see the lights creep up the rise of highway, the VW's engine sounding like a sewing machine stitching the night air together.

It's black dark, with only a slip of new moon in the sky. I swing a leg out in front of me like a blind man's cane to feel for the road, no more than a tentative path through the sage, and stumble along the ruts until the sage closes in around me. I pivot in a circle, straining to see some outline of camp against the horizon. There's only the sound of my feet shuffling dirt and, when I stop, the sound of a sheep bleating in the distance.

Fixing myself on that, I open my mouth and call out, "Lady, Lady, Laadeee!" into the night and then, louder, "Louise, Loueeeese! Hey girls, hey girls! Come on, come on, come ooon!" my voice warming and nearly singing into the black night. I stop and listen. A coyote yips in reply, and I hear an uneasy stir of bleating, then more silence.

I call out again, this time feeling the lonesome rising up through my body and echoing in the night, and I cry out harder to lose it, to make myself heard. "Pretty, pretty, giiirls, come ooon!" I think what it must feel like to stand in an opera house and sing the passion up into the farthest seats and warm the blood of an entire audience. How it must turn a person inside out to be able to do this.

A minute goes by, two.

And then here they are, out of the dark and suddenly upon me, in my face with their rough tongues and panting breaths, squeaking with delight at our reunion. From my pockets, I pull out the wax-paper wrapping of meat scraps and bread soaked in drippings and divide the treasure into their mouths. I hold them close against me and think I could almost lay myself down and sleep in the sage, I'm so tired. I whisper into their necks, "I'm so sorry, girls, for what I'm about to do."

And then I rise up to my feet and yell down at them, "Go home! Go home! Bad dogs!" as if they're in big trouble, and stumbling blindly through the sage, let the dim shapes of their bodies lead me back to camp.

# MURDI

It's late June 1979. The chapel of the Lovell funeral home is small, dark paneled, and dimly lit, set neatly with rows of metal folding chairs, only a few of which are occupied. I've chosen a seat at the rear and sit down to collect my thoughts, to let my eyes adjust from the early evening light of high summer. A few faces turn to me, and I see a scattering of ranch hands and their wives, the winter sheepmen turned summer farmers and irrigators with neatly pressed shirts and pale scalps, their hats now in their laps. Lila sits near the front of the room with her two boys, cowlicked and freckled, sunburned with summer.

Several rows behind are John's aunt and uncle, well-dressed in dark suit and silk, who have managed the Lewis Ranch since the passing of Claude. In the front of the room, raised on a small platform and flanked by pillared candles and vases of white daisies, sits the coffin of the herder Fred Murdi, smoky bronze, gleaming with polish and substance. Beneath its open lid, Fred's body lies on tufted ivory silk, only his profile visible to me, but clearly and curiously transformed from the man I've known.

I first met Fred in the spring of 1977 outside the Lovell lambing sheds, his bent figure leaning over water troughs with a hose while ewes lipped at the fresh water. His wiry arms and legs were covered in plastic bags and flannel that he'd secured with bits of twine and duct tape. Over this tattered arrangement he wore a large black oilfield rain jacket, spider-webbed in gray duct tape, with a hood from which he peered. He turned to me with a raised hand and a crinkled, gold-edged grin, his face smeared with a quarter inch of opaque goo later identified as Bag Balm, a medicated salve meant for chaffed cow and sheep udders. His lips were plastered with what I would discover were the membranes peeled from hard-boiled eggs, to protect his lips from the sun and weather.

"Ah, missy!" His voice a hoarse whisper. "You must be the lady!"

Fred's spring range in the northern hills near the Montana border was far from mine in the McCullough Peaks, but in the next two summers we shared boundaries both on the ranch's private lands on Little Mountain and on the federal grazing permits in the Big Horn National Forest. In the close quarters of our lush Little Mountain ranges, we visited as we kept watch between our two bands. He'd bring me his old copies of *U.S. News & World Report,* which he proudly read from cover to cover and generally saved in bundles under his bed. And after we trailed up to the big mountain, I might glimpse his silhouette on the far horizon of Rooster Hill. Born in the Basque country that runs along the common mountainous borders of France and Spain, he'd herded sheep all his life and had come to America with his brother and, in 1938, had hired on with the Lewis Ranch, where he's been ever since.

Fred died at his sheep camp from a leg wound he'd poulticed with fresh sheep manure and hidden from John when he came to tend his camp. "When he went to see the dentist, he got so excited you'd a thought he was goin' to see the queen of England," John said. "But the poor bugger wouldn't set foot near a hospital. He thought that's where you went to die."

This evening, with my sheep safely trailed to Roundup Springs on the flanks of Little Mountain and ready to hit the slide-rock trail at dawn, John had stayed at my camp and let me bring his pickup in to town for my "woman things" and to attend Fred's rosary service the evening before his funeral. "Just get the hell back here by dark with that pickup," he'd said as I drove away, " 'cause I got to carry his coffin tomorrow and get him buried."

It had been April, back at the Lovell lambing sheds, when I'd last seen Fred. John was about to haul Fred's camp out next day to his spring range on the Montana border and asked me to drive him into town to see the dentist. Fred had emerged from the dark jumble of his sheepwagon shading his eyes, dressed carefully for his trip to town in a brand-new pair of pinstriped overalls, a nearly crisp Pendleton wool shirt, and an unblemished pair of five-buckle overshoes. His "dentist outfit," according to John, and what he wore for his twice-yearly trips to Dr. Welch come rain, snow or summer's heat.

"You're looking mighty handsome today, Fred," I offered with more than a little astonishment.

"Oooh!" he nearly crowed in his Basque accent, "Every time I look in the mirror I look more old and more crumbly. But thank you." Fred was soft-spoken. His hands rose up in vivid exclamation as he told a story, but his words were never really more than a loud whisper.

On that day, his wagon was one of seven backed up and set against a woven wire fence facing the cottonwood river bottom east of the lambing sheds. "Wagon City" to the herders, this was their home during the late-winter months when the ewes were brought in to lamb, and I saw that he'd begun to pack for the upcoming trip to his spring range near the Montana border. For Fred, that meant corralling into gunnysacks the piles of string, cans, and rags that he'd collected over the winter and stored beneath the wagon. Even in normal times, his bed in the back was piled so high with boxes that he slept sitting on a five-gallon bucket by the woodstove, his body leaned back against the cupboards. That next morning, when John hooked the wagon to his pickup for the trip to the hills, it would be stuffed to the ceiling with Fred's treasures.

At his wagon door, Fred had turned, clumsy in his overshoes, to sort out the odd bits of orange baling twine beneath his feet. "Oh, give it up," he crooned to the strands that wouldn't let go of his buckles. His fingers were gnarled and slow, but I waited until he nodded that he was ready.

Perched on the seat of the ranch pickup with his hands in

his lap, he seemed out of place but happy. He wasn't a drinking man, like many of the other herders who frequented the bars, so those trips to the dentist were the social highlights of his year.

Leaning toward me, he looked out the window past my face and tapped his front teeth with a black fingernail. "These are all mine," he said, shaking his head at the cottonwoods alongside the road. "I don't neglect what's mine." Across the bridge of his nose, his glasses were taped together with electrical tape, and one gold tooth shone from his mouth as he spoke.

When I helped him through the door into the sterile white dentist's office, it felt like guiding an emissary from some exotic country, though there was no building or community— even the other nine herders, including myself, who worked for the Lewis Ranch—where he'd seem to belong.

Afterward, I asked if there were any other place in town that he might like to go, the hardware store or the mercantile, perhaps for a cold soda or an ice cream. "I just want to go home, please," he said. Back at his wagon, I helped him down from the pickup, and with a voice tired but almost lilting to song, he thanked me for my trouble. He maneuvered his hunched body around and, rearing back, pointed a knobby finger at the snow-covered Big Horns. "God willing, I'll see you on the big mountain," he whispered. Then he turned, looking at the ground in front of my feet. "Be careful out there, missy. It's no easy place."

The figure who rests before me in the coffin is someone I barely recognize. Fred's beard has been washed and clipped close. After years of being covered, the skin of his face is as clear and luminous as a young man's, and without his cobbled glasses, it appears even more so. He has been dressed in a crisply starched pale-blue shirt and a three-piece suit of light wool tweed, by any standard a distinguished presence.

For forty-one summers he'd herded sheep in the Big Horns northeast of Bald Mountain, a good and careful herder who seemed content with life just as it was. He never made more than a pittance of a salary, but by dressing in rags and banking his meager checks, he left over a hundred thousand dollars for his two final wishes. His first, according to John, was to be "buried like a banker," and his second was to leave the remainder to his brother in Casper to give to a local charity.

Around me now heads are bowed; a few hands are held. For this ragged and solitary man, a small community has gathered. I bow my head, too, and smooth the fabric of my flowered skirt against my legs, feeling the weariness of five days' trailing and the weight of losing Fred. I study my hands, cracked and rough and sooted black in the creases even though I'd scrubbed them.

*Who would gather here for me?*

The priest says words above our bowed heads, but I hear only the sound of his voice, familiar in a way that makes my heart cave with loneliness. Early light will find me horseback again, picking the trail up through rocks and gullies to a mountain that has come to feel like something I know, its endless silence both a balm and a curse. Now the voice of the priest settles around me, fitting my shape. I long to lie down, a fawn in the grass, to disappear, to say no to the mountain even though I've made my promises. Before me candles flicker and sputter.

Shards of light reflect from the coffin's gleaming surface. Inside, the body bears the trappings of the spirit's last wish, revealed here to this small world for a few brief hours. Others rise to leave, but I cannot. To hide the tears, I bow my head as though in prayer, and maybe that's what this is, but regardless, the other mourners pass me by with only a touch on the shoulder, and I don't have to explain myself. I hear the sound of shoes on carpet, the creaking of wood beneath, the rustling of fabric against fabric. I know that I have come to the end of this trail but don't know how it is that one returns home.

## ON THE DIAMOND TAIL

It was January 1990, and in the early afternoon, the thermome-
ter registered zero and the sun sent weak fingers of light
through the south-facing windows of our thin-walled house.
My husband had been out behind the tack shed all morning,
splitting blocks of pine that he'd hauled off the Big Horns in
eight-foot lengths through the heat of Wyoming summer. It
was his ritual, up the mountain in the morning to saddle a
horse from the cow camp pasture, then ride his circle of cattle
and shoe what horses needed to be shod that day. In the heat of
the day, he'd linger above Shell Canyon and cut a pickup load

of wood, then chug down the steep grades in low gear and stop at the bar for beers by midafternoon. When I got home from my forest-service job, he'd greet me at the door with a fresh cup of coffee and a cheery smile, his eyes glassy, his breath sharp with the smell of Listerine. Through the summer, the log pile grew into a wild and disorderly snake of wood dumped haphazardly from the back of his battered Chevy pickup.

Even in the brittle cold, the freshly split pine gave off the summer smell of pitch and forest duff as Joe stacked armload after armload in neat ricks on the east end of the front sunporch. Wood stacked three-deep and head-high made the world seem right with order and the promise of warmth no matter how far the temperature dropped. A couple weeks before, on New Year's Day, we'd sat on the couch with the fire crackling in the stove and agreed to have a child together. "If you'll just have it, I'll take care of it," he assured me when I wondered out loud how I could afford not to work. It was unnamable to me what was missing from our lives, but the promise of a baby sparked the emptiness. I imagined a baby to be the flesh that was missing from the bones of our marriage.

I fixed myself a cup of tea and went out onto the porch to breathe in the bright fragrance of split wood. I stood in the doorway and noticed the light slanting through the windows and how it left thick bars of gold across the river rocks of the hearth. We'd gathered the rocks by hand from the gravel banks of Shell Creek, turning each one over in the water to reveal its color, and now I could see veins of green and pink and glittering mica shooting through round granites, smooth as eggs.

This house was for each of us our first home. It had begun with a photograph on the front page of the Greybull paper, a photograph of a late-twenties bungalow with overhanging eaves and a sunporch with banks of latticed windows. The caption had read, "House without a Home," and I couldn't take my eyes away from it. The house had sat on Main Street in town and had been auctioned off for $180 when the high school enlarged its campus. A mover had been hired to haul it to Tensleep, but this was foiled by something—a bridge, maybe, or a change of heart—so for six months the house was parked by the railroad tracks, beached on top of beams and wheels. I made daily visits, climbing up into it to peel back carpets and imagine bare oak floors. Finding evidence of hobos sheltering there, I began worrying about fires with the propriety of ownership. I called the house mover and within days had written him a check for three thousand dollars, which covered the cost of the house and of moving it. Within weeks, my husband had negotiated a barstool deal on six acres of land along Beaver Creek at the foot of the Big Horns, and we had the pieces of our first home.

I sipped my tea and thought about what I'd wear to the party that night, the new dress ordered from J.Crew catalog for Christmas, thin black fabric with small red and green flowers, close fitting and elegant. It made me feel like someone else, pretty, like I might have stepped from the pages of a different world. I imagined this slim black dress over a belly with new life, maybe even then, and thought that lives are like stories and that this one might add up, might mean something after all. I pulled out the iron and ironing board and waited for the steam to rise up, hissing, while I traced the tiny flowers with my fingers. In the kitchen I heard the refrigerator door open, close, and another can of beer being cracked open. I remember thinking it was all beginning too soon, the drinking, and that by the time we left, for a fiftieth-birthday party at the Diamond Tail Ranch, he'd already be gone, three sheets to the wind. I knew the signs and had been charting my daily course by them for seven years.

He whistled through the living room with a beer in hand and another two pocketed in his vest, going out to split more wood. He grinned at me, his smile already an electric buzz across his face. "You can never have too much wood in this country!" He leaned over at the door to pull on heavy felt-pack boots and put on a wool scotch cap. He was cheerful. Snorting with delight. Beaming.


The ranch house is a gracious old log home, sprawling and generous, set in the bare-branched cottonwoods of Shell Creek. In the deep winter dusk, the windows shimmer in clusters of light. Against them, the snow-covered fields and the sky are dimmed into one immense thing, muted grays losing light and color, the sky not yet gone to stars. Inside, coats are already piled in the guest bedroom by the back door, and boots and overshoes have been deposited in pairs across the mudroom floor. I climb the stairs behind my husband and feel at once the heat of the party, the elbow-to-elbow energy of people sprung out of a winter jail of heavy coats and bitter cold.

"Hey, you bounder!" Joe enters the logjam of people in the kitchen and leans into each conversation with his big grin and a slap on the back. "Goddamn it, Marvin!" His eyes are loose and unfocused. "Jesus Christ!" He disappears into the crowd in the front of the house, toward the makeshift bar set up in the music room. I find a corner of bench at the crowded kitchen table and sit, a spectator to conversations.

At midnight, I wait in the passenger seat of the brown Toyota, my knees pressed together in the cold and the remains of a broccoli casserole held in a covered dish in my lap. From the dark carport, I can see people inside laughing, telling stories still. Some are reaching their arms into coats and saying their good-byes.

A man staggers out to my car, opens the driver's door, and lands hard in the seat. "Goddamn, my hat! Where's my goddamn hat?" Looking toward the house, not at me, he lurches back inside and through the door, his figure passing out of sight, and the whole dark world is silent again, every single living thing hunkered down in the cold. I think of the birds that sleep with their heads tucked under their wings and imagine being asleep in my bed under soft down. I hunker down, too, pulling the collar of my jacket up around my neck and pressing it to my ears and wait until my husband returns, his hat pulled down close over his eyes.

The driveway is nearly a mile long, with a sharp elbow where it corners a fenced field. Tonight the snow's packed and glazed into ice by the warmth of tires spinning across it. The barbed wire lining the lane glitters, hard frosted, in our headlights. As we turn from the house out into the lane, the car spins slightly by the gateposts, and I want to say that we're going too fast, but nothing comes out. I notice the grip of his hands on the wheel and the set of his jaw as we pick up speed. I open my mouth again and say words that come out a whisper, a whine, and they hang frozen in the air. His face turns on me in a hard glare, his eyes bulging, and he jams his foot down on the gas. We careen down the icy chute, the CorningWare lid rattling in my lap, the sound of tires on frozen ground like a ship tearing through ice.

At the turn, the car spins through the snow and into the air, almost silent as we leave the ground, but then out of jaws unhinged to the sky comes a siren of a wail. The Toyota slams into the far side of the irrigation ditch, and then it's silent again except for a wide-open voice yelling seven years of hard-jawed silence, maybe thirty-five years of silence, out into a night sky crackling with cold and vast enough to hold it.

Finally there is only the sound of warm metal ticking itself back into the cold. I wipe broccoli and cheese from my lap and climb out of the car and up from the ditch on shaky legs onto the graveled lane, where cows stand staring, curious, their whiskers frozen into white halos around their mouths. A half mile away, I can see the lights of the ranch. To the east, above the Big Horns, a lantern of winter moon has risen, and I strike out toward it, my feet rising lightly.

In this community of neighbors, there is little to hide and no one who doesn't understand a wife walking the road home in the night, so when a car stops, I get in and let them take me home. Upstairs, I find the girls asleep. Jenny, eight, her dark braids wild across her pillow as though stopped in motion, a somersault in her dreams. I pull the comforter up to her neck and brush her bangs from her eyes. I cross the room, picking up a half-eaten bowl of popcorn from the couch where they'd been watching movies. I turn off the lamp and let my eyes adjust to the moonlight flooding in through the east window onto Amy's bed. She's eleven, her hair golden, as her dad's was as a boy. I wonder that she can sleep so deeply in light so bright it nearly calls her name through the glass, through the splintered crystals of ice that frame it. I sink to a corner of her bed and lay a hand on her legs. They have been aching lately, growing pains. I straighten her covers and listen to her breathing and think that it sounds like the ocean giving itself up to the shore and taking itself away. *Here . . . away. Here . . . away.* I smooth the covers over her legs and understand that I've been wrong about many things.

How can I be enough for these precious girls, their mother long in her grave and their father drunk in a ditch on a winter's night? Who would be the flame for them if tonight I just kept walking? Where would I find forgiveness if I left?


I'd come to the Diamond Tail Ranch by chance in the winter of 1980, a single woman looking to rent the small cinder-block house by the cattail marsh. Stan said he could probably use me the six weeks during calving if I wanted to work nights checking the first-calf heifers. I said okay and stayed on for six years.

My shift would run from midnight until noon the next day, checking the heifers through the night, doing the morning chores around the corrals and helping to feed hay to the cattle. "Come on over to the corrals about seven tomorrow morning," Stan had said, "and we'll show you the lay of the land in the daylight." When I arrived, he was adjusting the heavy oiled harnesses on a pair of blond Belgian draft horses, Pet and Maude, as they ate their morning oats at the hitching rack of a low-slung log barn with horse corrals off to the left. On the right, a heavy timbered loading chute was wedged between the barn and a working alley with tall swinging gates that could be adjusted to cut cattle or horses into any number of corrals and pens. Stan introduced me to Chon Gonzales, his hired man, who'd just come up from spreading flakes of hay into the feed-bunks of the corral below the barn. "These horses, they like to run," he said for my benefit, but looked to Stan, teasing, instead. He wore brown insulated coveralls and had hair that curled black and glossy. Stan grinned and said, "Oh, I bet they've got over it by now." Pet and Maude had been out to pasture ever since the spring before, when their job of hauling hay to the winter cattle was done. A buyer was coming to look at them in a couple days, he said, and he wanted to get the kinks worked out of them. He slipped the snaffle bridles over their huge heads, snapped them into the yoke, and led them back to where the hay wagon sat backed into an open shed, already loaded with a few bales and a pile of feed cubes, or "cake," as he called it.

Stan backed the team up to the flatbed wagon with a high slatted front, slipped the wagon tongue into the yoke, and asked me to hold the horses while he snapped their harnesses into the traces. I stood before them, one hand raised up to each snaffle bit, as he gathered the longline reins into his hand and said, "Now, you just hold 'em while I step on the wagon; then we'll be in business." He sounded like he was swallowing a grin. Pet and Maude shifted their weight from side to side and grabbed nervously at the metal in their mouths. As he reached for the wagon stay to pull himself up, I wondered briefly if, in fact, I was supposed to be able to hold them. With the first creak of Stan's weight on the wagon, the horses lifted their front ends from the ground in unison, as though preparing for takeoff. I was lifted with them and in an instant eyed the alternatives—an old pickup with rounded fenders on one side and a hay rake bristling with spiky teeth on the other. As they lunged into the traces, they flung me off in front of the pickup and bolted with Stan, Chon, and the wagon in tow. Sprawled in the dirt, I watched them take the first corner by the horse corral, hay bales and cake bouncing off the bed like popcorn.

At midnight, the corrals were close with the heavy breathing of heifers bearing a great pregnant weight. After a week of working nights, they'd grown used to me. I could walk through them, weaving a path around their beached bodies, and they wouldn't move. I practiced walking quietly, making no fuss, though I carried a flashlight and completed a survey of their rear ends as I made the rounds. I looked for signs of labor, for the tail held high and kinked off to the side or maybe already the tips of hooves showing out from between the loose folds of vagina. When the calf was backward, the hooves appeared oddly, tips pointed down and the flat surface of hoof facing up. It was my job to walk the laboring heifer through the corrals— outsmarting her will to dive back into the darkest corner—and into the alley, where I'd close a gate behind her and steer her more quietly into the confines of the calving shed.

These nights were silent spaces, buckets dipped into a dark well and brought up one by one into wakefulness. Stan had pulled a sheepwagon down by the corrals so there was a place to build a fire and close off the cold, but usually the door stood wide open to the sounds of the night. I spent the winter nights zipped up in insulated coveralls and pack boots, protected from the raw cold of the corrals and, in the warmth of the sheepwagon, swaddled enough to fall into immediate sleep between rounds.

Sleep became the comma between things, thinly separating dreams from reality. I emerged from twenty-minute naps and carried my dreams out to find the world a changed place— a heifer showing two feet, an owl hooting from the cotton-woods on the lower side of the bull pen, northern lights spread shimmering across the sky in heartbeats of light, a wide swath of prayer rising up.

Every season was different, every year the same. I loved the order, the ritual, the immediacy of what needed to be done. I felt useful and in place. Winter mornings, I flaked hay into the corrals at dawn and heaved the harnesses onto the mules, Merle and Pearl, or the new draft horses, Bud and Barney. I saddled a colt for my own morning rounds of cattle in the field and later joined Stan and Mary on the far feedgrounds to flake off the hay and load the next day's bales onto the wagon. There was always a thermos of coffee covered in fine alfalfa leaves and sometimes a morning brownie. There was winter sun or blowing snow. There were jokes, sometimes poetry and philosophy, and there were always the geese coming back to the stubble fields in the late winter.

. . .

One night as I read by lamplight, I heard the crunch of boots on snow, a light knock on the side of the sheepwagon, and a man's soft voice. "Hello? Are you there?" He appeared at the open door, flakes of new snow sifting down and lighting on his hat, his shoulders. "I hope I'm not bothering you."

"No, not at all. Come in."

But he wouldn't, said only that he'd been up and thought he'd check to see if I needed help with anything. And that he'd just finished a book, essays by William Kittredge; did I want to read them?

I said yes and took the paper grocery bag he offered me, folded around the hard kernel of the book. "Well, goodnight," he said, and was gone into the sifting snow.

He had come to the ranch that fall, with my friends Gretel and Press, as part of the crew come to help gather cattle from the mountain pasture and trail them to the deeded ground at White Creek. I was told that he'd lost his wife just six months before in a horse accident down in the Texas Panhandle and that his daughters, then only six months and three and a half, were living with her mother and father up in Minnesota. He'd followed them up there and tried his hand at logging in the dark north woods to be with them, but something had broken, and he'd come west to be with his old friend Press here in Wyoming. Most of what I knew about him, I'd heard from someone else.

He'd fit right in and was good help, working behind the cattle quietly, respectfully. He laughed at other people's jokes but held himself apart, taking up little space. When it seemed he might stay awhile, Stan and Mary offered him a bed in the cookhouse behind the main house, and in return he rode colts, fixed fence, did odd jobs. He had little with him in this stopover of his life: a new Chevy pickup and horse trailer, a saddle, photographs of his wife and daughters, a substantial shelf of books. I discovered that he read widely and deeply, had studied literature in college. *More here,* I thought, *than meets the eye.*

Evenings, the pickup would head out the lane for town and would arrive back in the early-morning hours, parked askew. Mornings, he would appear at the ranch breakfast table early for coffee, quiet and polite, cleaning his wire-rimmed glasses on a shirtsleeve with no words about the night before.

One full-mooned night down at the corrals, I stood looking out across the silvered pasture where the heifers were turned out during the day, several acres between the corrals and the house, the long side on the banks of Shell Creek sheltered by bare-branched old cottonwoods. I stood in the perfect stillness of night and imagined walking across that empty field in the moonlight to enter the cookhouse quietly, like a thief, and go to the bed of the sleeping man whose daylight face was smooth as a still pond. Bare skin, the ripples of grief. I could have sliced in and out like a knife, and in the dark of night it would be as though it had never happened.

Morning. Every season is different, every year the same. At dawn, I saddle a young bay gelding called Tuck who's been known to leap sideways through the air when a cow turns on him. He has fancy Doc O Dynamite breeding, which makes him quick and athletic, but he appears to be afraid of cattle. Tim, Stan and Mary's elder son, has turned him over to me for these long, hard trots through the willows at dawn and dusk, checking for new calves, hoping that the miles and cattle will help him outgrow it. I check my coat pocket for notepad and pencil, my saddlebags for scour pills and penicillin, and pull myself up into the saddle, burdened with the layers of early morning.

We skitter across frozen ground at a dicey trot, then line out through the snow at a steady pace as we warm up to each other and the job at hand. We move past the house and out through the field to the east past the old sheep sheds and slow to a walk as we fall off the slope into Shell Creek.

The willows plume in frost-rimmed clumps along the meadows on the far side of the creek. Hidden among them, scattered, are the mixed-breed cows of the grade herd, older, seasoned, able to calve on their own given any shelter from wind and snow. I ride them dawn and dusk. When they're calving heavy, I ride them at noon as well, looking for new calves, making sure they've sucked, writing down the mother's number to make the calf's tag, looking for illness, for cows on the wrong side of the fence, for trouble. This morning a skiff of new snow brightens the ragged remains of the last storm. At a long trot we snake through paths in the brush, making our intricate circle of the most hidden places, the backsides of willow clumps, the long narrow irrigation ditch that could trap a cow on her back during labor or keep a calf from climbing out.

I'd come to the Diamond Tail fresh from the sheep ranges and knowing nothing about cattle, so everything I learned over six years was thanks to Stan and Mary, from being asked the hard questions day after day, stitching the threads between birth and death. "Didn't you see her bag was swollen? Couldn't you tell she'd dropped a calf? You have to pay attention. Don't you see that cow off in the corner looking out into the hills? Can't you see that there's something just wrong there? Pay attention."

Last night's squall has brought new calves. A black baldy calf up and suckling its mother. The cow licks the calf's hind end furiously, possessively, then swings her head up high in defiance of me. Tuck trembles and shifts his weight from foot to foot, bunching his weight on his hindquarters and looking for an escape from the cow's glare. Pulling out my notebook and pen, I huddle over the saddle horn, holding him in place long enough to write the number of the mother cow, the sex of the calf and that he's sucked. Through the willows and along the fence, five new calves are wobbling bright eyed in the snow.

Trotting around the upper fence between the pasture and the sagebrush hills beyond, I notice a cow watching me from the corner above the haystack. Her look says she has something to hide, so we pull the hill at a trot, Tuck's breathing now almost a snort, a slight vapor of heat rising up off his body. I'm warming up, too, in the pale sun under all these clothes, the ragged silk scarf wound around my neck smelling of stale breath and sweat. As the light spreads across the sage, I'm suddenly tired and want only to be done with this round, the uncertainty behind every bush.

She is a black Angus and stands facing us as we approach. At her feet is a calf sprawled in the shape of birth, the mucous and afterbirth covering its nose indicating that it never breathed. The ground around the calf is trampled, the snow and frozen earth chopped up with worry. The cow lowers her head to the calf, billowing her nostrils toward us and switching her tail in defiance. Her tongue shoots out and roughs the flank of the stillborn calf as though urging it once more to get up, get up. She swings her head back at us, her eyes dark, fierce pools, then lifts it and bellows up into the air.

I unwrap the lariat strapped to my saddle horn and slide to the ground, asking myself all the questions that I know I'll hear. *Hadn't you noticed her? What was she doing last night when you rode? Was she off by herself? Goddamn, another calf.*

I pick the loop off the end of the coil and shake out a little rope. Behind me Tuck's pulling back against the reins and in front of me the cow's snorting, stomping, switching her tail angrily. "Hey, Momma," I say softly, "hey hey hey. You lost your sweet baby." The words come out a croon, like a love song, and I hope she doesn't knock me over. "Hey, Momma, we'll find you another baby; yes we will." With my free hand I lift the calf's hind legs and with the toe of my boot work the loop of rope over the raised back hooves and down around its hind end, then lift the hind feet higher and let the loop drop around the stiff flanks of the dead calf. I pull the loop snug and back away, paying the rope out in front of me.

"Hey, pretty pretty." Now I'm talking to Tuck, hoping that he'll let me mount him again with the rope in my hand. "This is no big deal pretty, pretty boy, and you can do the right thing here. Easy easy easy." I have the reins in one hand and the rope in the other. If he'll stand firm, we can do this, but instead he jumps as I get on, and the rope pulls from my hand and drops to the ground. I slide back off, pick it up, and drape it as high as I can in a clump of greasewood brush. I lead Tuck some distance away from the cow and turn him to face her, then climb up in the saddle as he stands, trembling. "Easy easy easy. This is no big deal, baby." I trick him back to where I can lean down and pick the rope out of the greasewood, holding it loosely away from me in case he jumps. With my thumb straight up and out of the way, I take two quick dallies around the horn, and when Tuck lurches forward, the calf bumps behind us on the end of the rope.

The cow lets out a deep bellow and charges after her calf, frantically licking at its head, stepping on its front legs dragging stiffly behind, and when she does, the rope catches and jerks us back. The cow whirls and leaves us for the spot where she birthed her calf, as though he might still be there and maybe this time rise up on wobbly legs to butt at her side. We wait, Tuck trembling and in a lather. I raise my voice into a keen, "Whah-whah-whah," like a calf crying out, until she finds us again and covers the carcass with her rough tongue. The reins loosen. Then there's the thud of hooves on snow, the creak of leather, the rope stretching slightly as it tightens. We head back for the barn, across the frozen creek, across the snowy fields, the dead calf's body shushing and bumping behind us, the bellowing cries of the mother announcing our return.

I met Joe's daughters in 1983 in that season between winter and spring when the ranch was old snow, bare trees, and dead grass. Jenny was a year and three months old, Amy was four and a half. Their Norwegian grandparents and their mother's older sister had brought them from Minnesota, all scrubbed and loved, to the ranch to see their dad, who was enduring the time of his mourning in tight-lipped stoicism. As Stan and Mary and I introduced ourselves, the sense of loss felt fresh, as though a wave had just washed over them and taken their skins. It had only been nine months, and the grandmother's hair had fallen out with grief, her head now wrapped in a scarf. I noticed her swollen eyes and eyebrows arched as if in perpetual surprise at what life had brought to her door. I thought about a stone skipping across water, about lives touching down. I shook hands with the grandmother, her hands only bone. Nine months is the time it takes to grow a baby, but how much time does it take to lose a child?

They'd been there less than an hour when I followed them down the rutted lane to the small round corral behind the barn where Joe wanted to show the girls a baby calf. Jenny, who hadn't strayed more than a few feet from her grandmother since their arrival, was hitched up in her arms, an exact image of pictures I'd seen of her mother, olive skin and dark wispy hair poking out from beneath a pink knit cap. Amy stayed beside her father, her hand up in his, and I noticed she walked just like him, as tall as she could make herself and with a tough little stride, determined to keep up. Her grandmother had braided her long blonde hair tightly, which seemed to pull her face into something wide open and bright, hopeful when she turned to look up at her dad.

I still believed then that I could hold myself apart and simply watch. That love was reasonable, something that could be chosen. What I didn't know was that these girls would be my gift.

The Sunday before, Joe had pulled up in front of my house with a horse in his trailer. "He's fast, bred for it. They're racing up by the Greybull airport this afternoon. Come ride him." Simple as that, I said yes and loaded my saddle in the back of the pickup, adding that I'd have to be back for the evening rounds. "I'll get you back," he said, and we were gone.

The track was a quarter-mile stretch marked off alongside the airport runway, fifteen miles west of the ranch. At one end was a starting gate with six stalls, even though these were stock-saddle races, casual and Western, for anybody with a horse and the ten-dollar entry fee. Next to the track there were bleachers with people, kids, and dogs milling around and a table where wagers were being made. The day was raw, the wind up. Clouds sailed past the face of the Big Horns. Across the basin sixty miles to the west, the Absarokas lay covered in snow.

Joe helped shorten my stirrups and gave me a leg up onto the tall bay gelding, and I set off at a trot to warm him up and get the feel of him. Away from the crowd, I let him out into a canter and felt a slow smile creep to my face. The bright wind, the long-legged horse, the thoughtful attention of another person doing something to make me happy. By the time we'd stepped into the starting gate and felt it close behind us, my heart was pounding in my ears and I hoped I wouldn't fall off. I held the saddle horn with one hand and with the other grabbed a handful of mane and waited. The last horse loaded, the gates flew open and we were off in a wild thunder down the track, clods of dirt pelting my face.

We placed fourth out of six, but the exhilaration of the ride spread into my arms and my heart and opened up a place for the man who so quietly had seen to this happiness. Adjusting stirrups, a leg up, what are these things to make a space for tenderness? When we stopped at the bar for a drink, I looked him full in the face for the first time since we'd met six months before.

Back at the ranch barely by dusk and almost too late, he helped me back on the long-legged horse with the short racing stirrups for my evening ride across the creek, my skin warm with alcohol and his attentions. I rode the circle nearly in the dark, peering into the brush, happily splashing back through the creek at a trot. When I returned in the dark, in the deepening cold, I found that he'd waited and fixed me a plate of food. After I ate, he held my hand and asked, "Have you ever thought about getting married?" I shook my head, and then he asked softly, "If you ever do, would you think about me?"

## GATHERING

---

There was a time in my life when I thought I lived at the center of the universe—would, in fact, say that I did—because I thought everything I needed was within arm's reach: friends, horses, family, a sense of place, and a job to do. It didn't last for long. Likely, it's never meant.

It's all about quiet when the diesel pickups are shut off and the horses are unloaded and we're horseback in the dim morning light, sent out to follow a bare ridge to its end. Riders and horses have been dropped off along the road, and those that remain are sent in a scatter from the trailers to ride the first part of the morning alone. Meadowlarks are singing down in the draws and the range smells sweet and damp with morning. My horse feels good and fresh, but I hold him to a careful trot so he can cover the miles to where I'll begin to pick up cattle. Though I can't feel it yet, I know that when the sun rises, the day will turn scorching hot, and it's my job to help him last through to dark.

As daylight comes, I see the shapes of riders and dogs in the distance, sometimes only dots on the horizon, and I'm not sure who's on what ridge, but I know they'll find the cattle they're meant to find and bring them on.

I imagine that in their solitude they might be singing to themselves as I sometimes do, softly, because my voice is not good and because the morning's quiet is large. And because it's large, they might be considering their lives as I sometimes do when I'm riding alone. When I look up again, they've disappeared from the horizon, fallen below into draws and hidden pockets to begin the gather. I reach the top end of my country and find cattle there, a handful of pairs bedded down in a green swale. A sleepy calf raises its head, blinking in surprise to see the strange creature of me, but the cows know it's time. They've been waiting. They gather their calves up, bawling softly, and head down the trail.

It's still black-dark morning, four o'clock in the Shell Valley, late June, and just enough rain's spitting from the sky to muddy the windshields. We pull across the highway onto the

Red Gulch road with two gooseneck trailers and an old Suburban with a four-horse behind, all loaded heavy with saddle horses and gear. Packed into these outfits are the dozen or so hands and help from both ranches, the Diamond Tail and the G-O, whose cattle run in common in the hills and up on the forest reserve. We pull to the roadside and watch, bleary-eyed, as the headlights of Steve's rig approach, coming the highway from Shell. In the crush of bodies and slickers in the backseat, I check my jeans pocket for lip balm and hope my chaps and bridle made it into the back of the pickup, somewhere beneath the four dogs and the pile of lunch coolers. It is 1985, my last full summer as a hand on the Diamond Tail Ranch.

By the time Steve pulls alongside, the rain's coming down in earnest and the wind has picked up. The passenger window gets rolled down by one of his kids, and he leans across them, smoking, to the window. "Morning," he says.

"Morning." There's a pause, Stan chewing on a toothpick.

"You see cattle at Split Ear yesterday?"

"Three pair. Kicked 'em on down to Sulphur with another little package. Got 'em through the gate, so Sulphur should be clean."

There is another long pause in which it suddenly seems that we have all the time in the world. For all the early-morning urgency of scrambling and loading in the dark, we're now lolly-gagging at the highway as though having a casual afternoon chat. Now it's the rain that appears to be in question. Lord knows, it's not us they're worried about getting wet but the roads. Spring roundup depends on getting the rigs shuttled around miles and miles of dirt roads, all of which can turn to gumbo under a good soaking.

"May as well try for the top of Red Mountain and wait for daylight. See what this day looks like."

"Might pass over. We aren't meant to get it."

"May as well give 'er a try."

We pull all four outfits back onto the dirt road and begin the long washboard haul through the hills, chancing that we're under a cloud and not a storm. We doze these dark miles, past Dutch Springs and up the long, steady grade of Red Mountain. There, from on top and the high ridges beyond it, we'll scatter across the badlands to gather the cattle to Trapper Creek and start them up Black Mountain, the first step toward their summer on the Big Horns.

Red Mountain is an upturned slab of Chugwater Formation that rises, gradually and smoothly, out of the basin floor and ends in a high perch of red cliff from which a lot of country can be seen. It's all windblown grass and sage, no trees, so when we park in the dark, our rigs are the tallest things around, and over their dim silhouettes we can see the horizon of mountains to the east. The wind's blowing hard and the rain discouragingly steady. Mary pulls a thermos from the canvas bag at her feet and passes coffee around while we wait for first light.

"Am I seeing things?" she finally asks. "What on earth is that on the top of Steve's horse trailer?"

From the backseat, we peer into the dark, but truly it seems too early to care.

Mary is persistent. "It looks like . . . could it be—oh my gosh, I believe it's a chicken! It must've been roosting this morning when Steve drove off! It's come all the way from Trapper Creek on the horse trailer! In the rain!"

This catches our attention and we unfold, rumpled, from our close quarters and pull on the slickers we've been clutching in our laps. Those in the other rigs notice our movement, and suddenly we're all standing around Steve's trailer pondering the miracle of the chicken still roosted on a crossbar.

"Well, I'll be damned."

"That gal's had quite the ride."

"Maybe we ought to check the highway this evenin' for eggs."

"So what the heck do we do with her?"

With all the commotion and scary yellow slickers circled around her, she bails off, squawking, and flaps to the ground. Stan and Steve and half the kids go for their ropes, and then a rodeo commences. We're sliding and diving on the wet ground to catch that poor hen, who refuses to be roped, laughing to tears on a rainy mountaintop as daylight breaks.


Devils Leap, Trapper Canyon, Red Mountain, Sulphur, the Mesa, Red Gulch, Black Mountain, the Mail Trail Gap. You don't need to be a geologist to know this country is made from great slabs of earth punched and heaved up from below, then gouged into canyons and wrinkles from above. As though all this damage has just occurred, the slabs are scattered and tilted, their jagged edges exposed as cliff, with gray limestone up along the mountain face and the burnt red of the Chugwater Formation in the foothills below. Creased and broken, this is the country we are gathering. As morning comes, we look across it all and can see the storm is passing, that the day will come on clear and strong.

We gather through the early morning from the far reaches and high corners of the Mesa, Sulphur and Red Mountain down into the dry bowl of Red Basin. As it grows hot, the herd begins to take shape with cattle spilling down trails and out of draws, lonesome horses nickering with the joining of riders.

The pickups and trailers have been left down in the wide shallow basin alongside the dirt road where everyone will pass eventually. As we get close, we let the cattle drift and we go in search of cold water and hot coffee, maybe a candy bar from the cooler. The horses brighten to a trot, as though their day might be over, and for some it is. Stan, Tim, and Mary pull the saddles from their young colts, trading them for older, stouter horses who can take the hard work still ahead.

Mary cinches up her horse and tells me over her shoulder, "You better have a sandwich, too. It's a long ways to lunch."

Mary is a third-generation ranch woman who'd grown up one of three sisters on the Budd Ranch in the high, wide-open Big Piney country south of Jackson Hole. She claims that's real ranch country, too high and cold to grow crops. "I never had a fresh tomato until I went to college," she'd say when she asked me to make a salad. "I'm just much better with beef and beans and things in cans. When I married Stan and moved to Shell Valley, I wondered how in the world I ended up here in the middle of all these flatlander farmers. It took me a while to get used to the change."

She learned to work cattle with her sisters under the strict tutelage of her father, who believed that it was all to be done horseback and in only one way—quiet and smart.

"When you ride into a field, you start working that cow as soon as you walk through the gate. She knows. You can start to work her where you want her from a good distance. You can get a lot out of her without ever dashing around at a gallop or acting a fool, as my father would say."

And because we lacked the strength to manhandle the cattle and the skill to rope at a high run, she taught me how to get the job done without them.

"That number one sixty-one yellow-tag calf's looking better, but he's going to need another shot of penicillin. Let's pick up this little bunch of cattle here under the cottonwoods and work them over towards the upper gate. See now, this little guy just falls to the back of the bunch, and it's easy as pie to drop your rope on him. Just like this."

Mary is slight and wiry, with disturbingly blue eyes and a quick wit. For thirty years she has kept a daily journal of events—weather, cattle moves, visitors, geese coming back in the spring, notes about the kids, quotes from her poetry anthology on the shelf by the kitchen table.

"Do you write personal things?" I once asked her. "You know, feelings about your life?"

She laughed at the question but clearly had thought about the answer. "No." She shook her head. "I can look back at any given day and read between the lines. But when I die, that will all go with me."

. . .

I hold the candy bar in my teeth and tie the ham sandwich, cinched up like a butterfly in a baggie, into the leather strings below my saddle horn. No one on the Diamond Tail uses saddle bags or carries water with them, no matter how long the prospect of the day. I've come to understand that you're meant to be simply rider and horse, with as little extra flap as possible. When I first arrived at the ranch, Stan teased me about my sheepherder ways. He'd grin and say, "You got the goddamn kitchen sink tied on behind your saddle." My saddlebags quietly got left behind in the tack shed, and I began to find pockets instead for scour pills, syringes, notebooks and penicillin. I wanted to be just horse and rider, a neat little package that could travel light and work well. I had people willing to teach me. I wanted to learn from them and wanted to fit in.

The cattle are stringing out in the late morning, bound for the trails that lead to water down in the willows and sedges and lush grass of Red Gulch below us. It's Kelly and me and the Flitner kids now plodding along together behind the drag in the heat.

Kelly's face looks puffy and beat up and, under the shade of his black cowboy hat, slightly gray. He grew up in Shell Valley and for years has wandered back and forth between oilfields and ranches for his paycheck, rodeoing and partying notoriously in between, and always with a smart quip. One night along the way, he'd lost his wife and baby son in a trailerhouse fire that sprang up suddenly in the early hours. We all felt he was driven to his edges because of it.

"Closed down the Outpost last night and tried my damnd-est to get one of those sassy fillies in the chute before closin' time. Just an eight-second ride is all it woulda took. *Eeehaaaa!* I know I coulda rode 'er, rode 'er, rode 'er . . ."

He's nearly singing now, delighted with his words and swinging his rope out onto the backs of slow calves. He has a captive audience and is bent on shocking us, but we're long used to him and don't shock easily anyway. One summer Sun-day, he'd appeared on the porch of the Flitners' White Creek cow camp just as Father Camillus, a family friend and Benedic-tine priest, was about to conduct an informal outdoor mass before the day's work. Kelly was wearing his garish long-fringed rodeo chaps and heading for the coffeepot inside, but Father Camillus, ever the gentleman, had extended a light-hearted welcome.

"Is your spirit crying out for morning mass, Kelly? Would you give us the gift of your presence?"

"My spirit's cryin' out for caffeine and bacon."

"Well, Kelly, you know you are most certainly welcome," the priest said warmly, and then, with a twinkle in his eyes, "I've never seen a cowboy wearing . . . exactly what color would you call those chaps?"

Kelly stopped dead in his tracks, lit up and got his most earnest smile going. "Well, Father, guess I'd call 'em titty pink!" he roared, then ducked through the cabin door.

"Ah, Kelly, you are a treasure of God." Father Camillus just smiled and raised his hands to the rest of us, scattered among pine stumps and benches on the porch in the early-morning light, where we waited, spurs on our boots and coffee in hand, for a blessing.

We tried hard to not let Kelly get our goat or embarrass us, but the other feeling he could inspire in us was awe.

As the sun's heat settled on us in earnest, he started off again with his head thrown back and his rope circling through the air after nothing in particular as he began to recite poetry.

> There are strange things done in the midnight sun
> By the men who moil for gold;
> The Arctic trails have their secret tales
> That would make your blood run cold;
> The Northern Lights have seen queer sights,
> But the queerest they ever did see
> Was that night on the marge of Lake Lebarge
> I cremated Sam McGee.

He could quote page after page of Robert Service and often did during the slack times behind the cattle. There wasn't one of us whose jaws didn't drop in amazement at this side of him no matter how often we'd seen it. Regardless of how hard he'd partied the night before or how little sleep he'd gotten, he always showed up and always did his job. And, if we were lucky, we'd hear his poetry.

By noon the cattle are bunched on the water below the Red Gulch corrals, where my sheepwagon's parked. If this were our destination, we'd be done and it would've been a pretty fair day getting here, but this is only the first gathering point of several. We stand our horses around the cattle at an easy distance, letting cows and calves mother up for the hard push over the divide into the Trapper Creek drainage.

Tim rides up and drops his horse down into the creek beside me to let him water. Now in his early twenties, he's lanky and dark haired with his mother's eyes. He sits his horses quietly and tends toward an intense and solemn reserve.

Standing ankle-deep in the shallow, brackish water of Red Gulch, our horses drink their fill through the wiry sedges and horsetail that cover the bottom. Tim has just come back from taking one of his colts to a Ray Hunt clinic, so I ask him about it.

"It's all about making the right thing easy and the wrong thing hard. You let the horse make the decision to get himself into trouble or to get himself out of it. It's up to him."

"So what does that mean?"

"Well, take your reins and put just the slightest amount of pressure on his mouth, as little as you can."

I'm riding Chili, a solid-bred red roan quarter horse my husband had given me. He's a four-year-old gelding with plenty of cow in him, but under my heavy hand he's become a little stubborn. So I take the reins and barely squeeze the snaffle bit into the corners of his mouth. This irritates him, and he lets me know by tossing his head.

"Stay steady. Keep the pressure slight and even. You're making his world uncomfortable, and he's got to figure out how to make it okay again."

Chili gives his head another shake and then shifts his weight back from the bit, not quite taking a step.

"There! Give him slack now and rub his shoulder. You've

got to pay attention and feel the slightest change in him, reward that little bit of give. Keep that in mind and you'll have him backing across the arena with nothing but what you just gave him. Make the right thing easy and the wrong thing hard."

Tim and I had bonded early on in adversity. We'd been left in charge of the ranch on one of the rare occasions when Stan and Mary took a break to travel, usually after Christmas and before the crush of heifers calving in February. At the time, he was a skinny high school kid; I was eleven years older but still a green hand. We managed many things well, and I'm sure we were thanked and appreciated for it, but I remember best what went wrong.

It was winter and must have been a Saturday or Sunday because Tim was there to help feed. A cow was lying on the feedground with her uterus prolapsed out onto the straw and frozen ground. We saddled horses and herded her and her young calf gently down the lane and back to the corrals. She seemed able to walk all right, though slowly, and occasionally would stop and strain as if wanting to push it all out. In the calving shed, we locked her head into the stanchion, gave her a heavy dose of penicillin in the muscle of her hip, and washed the prolapse with a bucket of warm antiseptic water. Using all four hands, we worked the mass of it back inside her and held our hands flat against her hind end while she strained to undo our work.

"She needs sewed up," he said.

"Yes. Stan'll be home tonight, right?"

"Yes."

"Should we call a vet?"

We calculated the cost. This was the early eighties when interest was high and calf prices shockingly low, a time that many ranchers didn't survive and the ones who did took in hunters, contracted fencing jobs, cut corners and let pickups and paint grow old. That winter, with a quiver in his lip, Stan had asked me to take a fifty-dollar monthly pay cut to help make ends meet, and I said yes. The line between making it and losing it was that close, and we weren't about to call a vet frivolously. Smeared with blood and mucus, we leaned into her hind end and weighed our decision.

"So this is just a prolapse, right?," I ask. "We see it all the time on the mountain. A cow will have some of her uterus hanging out and it isn't pretty, but she doesn't die. Nobody gets too upset about it, do they?"

"No, we just get her into a corral, then cleaned up, sewed up and shipped to town to the sale."

"Is this the same?"

"It looks worse, maybe, but I think it's the same."

"I do, too." And after a long pause, I say, "All right, then. We'll wait for Stan?"

"Yeah, wait for Stan."

We broke a clean bale of straw for her and covered the stall with it. When we turned her loose, she lay down in it and pushed her uterus back out into the straw. When Stan got home that night and went to the barn to sew her up, she was already dead, her calf curled up in the straw at her side.

For days Tim and I hardly spoke, even to each other. It's hard to say which is the easier target for accumulated losses, the female hired hand or the eldest son. We both took it hard from Stan and held it heavy on our shoulders. Just for a couple of days, until it passed and the burden was shared once again among us all.

The Red Gulch corrals are graceful and old-fashioned, their cedar posts and poles wildly uneven, bent and gnarled into a kind of rangeland sculpture, parts of it with woven-wire fence, a remnant of the ranch's sheep days. This had been the site of what Joe and I called our "honeymoon" in the months before our July wedding. I'd pulled the ranch sheepwagon out to use as my spring camp, as I did every year in May when the cows first came out in the hills. It had been a special time for us, days horseback, evenings around a campfire, reading aloud to each other by flashlight in bed. Friends would brave the rough road from Trapper Creek on a Saturday night to share elk steaks and cold beer around the fire. Now, in the heat of summer, the camp looks forlorn and uninviting. By mid-July, both cattle and camp will move up to the forest permit at Granite Pass.

In my first season of calving, I'd worked six solid weeks before Stan said I could have the Sunday off, "if you'll just do chores and help us feed early." I was planning to drive through the hills to Crystal Creek, where I had a boyfriend, stay the night and come back early the next morning. I'd done the corral chores in the dim light, harnessed the team and picked Stan and Mary up at the house in the wagon to get our feeding done. Once that was finished and the horses had their noses deep in their grain, Stan looked off at the horizon and said, to no one in particular, "Well, let's just saddle up and bring those few pair down from the Bosch draw. Won't take long, then we'll get you outta here." I looked at my watch, and it was already eleven. I was tired and could feel the morning slipping away into afternoon, the tears gathering in pools behind my sunglasses. Stan took a long look, bewildered to see that his ranch hand was crying, then cleared his throat, struggled for the words to address this delicate situation, and asked, "Were you wanting the *whole* day off?"

I learned what I did from Stan because he believed I should be able to do anything that he could. This had little to do with my merits. He just needed good help, and if he didn't have it, he knew he had to make it. He expected the world from me, and only once in a great while did he ever get it.

"When you ride up through those cattle," he told me that morning, "you take a good long look over the whole outfit. If one of those cows is in trouble or hiding something, acting suspicious, you're gonna be able to see it from a mile away. If you're looking. You've gotta watch these cattle like they were your own."

Some lessons I learned all by myself, simply by making mistakes that could have killed me. The first summer at the Diamond Tail, my horse dragged me at the end of a lariat for a quarter mile at Granite Pass. I was camped at Big Springs, at the edge of the trees just off the highway to Sheridan and kept my horse on a picket line because there wasn't a corral. I'd been using Blue, a rangy Appaloosa who belonged to Gretel. He was a stout and dependable mountain horse under saddle but had one very bad habit: if he thought he had a chance to quit me, he'd whirl around and gallop off to leave me standing afoot. In the daily transitions from picket chain to bridle and back again, he began looking for opportunity to outweigh me.

That Sunday, Tom, my Crystal Creek boyfriend, was visiting and calmly said, "I'm going to teach this horse a lesson." He took my lariat, dropped the coil with the noose end to the ground and with the other end tied a no-slip bolon knot loosely around Blue's neck, then turned to me and said, "Now stand back out of the way." I stepped back but felt certain he was going to lose not only my horse but also my rope, so I moved forward to grab the coil for backup. In the sudden whirling and dust, next thing I knew I was on the ground behind Blue, at a high gallop, and headed for the barbed-wire highway fence with the noose of the lariat cinched tight around my upper left thigh. I had no knife to cut myself free, but with the rope so high on my leg I was able to hold my body upright and my head off the ground, at least for a while. Closing in on the barbed wire, I feared he'd jump and drag me through, but instead he veered to follow the gravelly trail alongside and across the open meadow.

I remember cars slowing down on the highway, a young boy staring through the open window with the straw of his cold drink nearly to his lips, watching, craning to see what was happening not ten yards away. I remember his face and thinking it might be the last I ever saw, and then he was gone. As we crossed the meadow, Blue tired and slowed to a hard trot, and I could hear his breath heaving with the load. I lost the strength to hold myself up and rolled over to my stomach, my mouth filling with the dirt and roil of the trail.

When I came to, there was a face asking me questions, fingers being held up in front of my eyes. Jack, the government trapper, and his wife, Mary, were stopping by the camp to visit when they'd come upon the accident. He said later that a doctor from New York, seeing it all unfold from the road, had the presence of mind to stop and climb through the fence and simply stand in the trail in front of the approaching horse. Blue wasn't mean, just scared and glad to have a reason to stop. The doctor tied him to a fence post and cut me loose just as Jack and Mary pulled up. Learning that Jack was an EMT, he'd handed me over and left, and I never got to thank him for saving my life. He'd tied Blue up thirty yards from the edge of the timber, where surely I would've broken apart.

Jack drove me down to the basin's emergency clinic, where they picked gravel out of me and gave me a healthy dose of codeine. I'd broken no bones but had raw open sores and had traumatized every muscle in my body. Tom brought me to Gretel, who put me to soaking in her bathtub and then piled blankets on me in her bed when I began shivering with shock in the August heat. The next day, when I still couldn't move, Tom drove me back up the mountain and deposited me at my old camptender's cabin to heal up in the cool mountain air, above the flies and mosquitoes of the basin. John, who'd helped me through many scrapes before, made up a soft bed on the living-room couch, and for a week I took codeine and slept, letting my body mend itself. Eight days later I was horseback again and back at work, with a two-inch foam pad between me and the saddle, on a tough little black Morgan named Thunder. Though my hind end healed soon enough, I was left with a dent in my left thigh and a deep and solemn respect for ropes.

Cresting the divide with the cattle, we can see the metal glint of pickups and trailers down in the bottom and riders coming up to meet us. My husband and some of the neighbors, having shuttled the rigs from Red Mountain back around the highway to the Trapper Creek Road, are riding up to help us on with the next leg of this journey.

Kelly whoops "Got 'er made now!" and tosses his rope out behind the calves, who jump down the hill with new-found energy. "Yes sirree. Forge ahead with neither fear nor judgment!"

We have the cattle headed to water, fresh help at hand and lunch waiting within sight. It's midafternoon and the cattle are streaming toward the snowmelt waters of Trapper Creek, one major hurdle passed and another to go at day's end when we push them up the steep pitch of Black Mountain and turn them loose to drift for the night.

I watch Joe and the girls come up the hill, edging around the cattle, and feel as though I haven't seen them for weeks. When I got up in the middle of the night, Joe made me coffee and promised to bring the girls along once he finished shoeing horses. He's got Jenny, four, riding on the back of his saddle with her arms locked around his waist. Her dark hair is in braids and under a ball cap, turned backward to keep it from bumping into her dad's back. Amy, seven, is on old Bill and fol-lowing close behind, her little red boots beating a rhythm to keep him from stopping. The girls spot me and start waving to catch my attention, as though I wouldn't be already looking for them. I wave back with a foolish grin, thinking, *This is my family.*

Since their mother's death, they've been living most of the year with her family in Minnesota, spending summers and Christmas here with Joe and me. This will change before long, and instead they'll spend their vacations back with their grandparents and aunts.

There will be times when I worry about the change, about them leaving the solid and predictable comfort of their grandparents' home for what can seem a disorderly life that changes with the seasons. I'll worry over my inadequacies and those of their dad. But this is the scene I come back to when I need to be reminded of what is meant to be.

Getting the cattle up Black Mountain will be the last challenge of the day. They're tired, and so are horses and hands. The trail's straight-up steep and west-facing, catching the full brunt of the afternoon sun, and there's more ground than should be covered in one day. But there's no place we can leave the cattle until we get them up and through the Black Mountain gate, where a fence will hold them. No matter how you cut it, it's just one of those days that starts in the dark and ends at dusk. For now, until it cools, we simply have to hold them in a bunch around the water and let them rest.

In the red-dirt flats, we trade off holding herd while the cows and calves mother up and settle. There aren't many places for them to go, hemmed in by the steep mountain face on one side and nearly circled by hayfield fences. On either side of the creek crossing, the banks are thick with willow and narrowleafed cottonwood, and spreading out from them is a tangle of chokecherry, buffaloberry, snowberry and skunkbush. We prepare to hunker down in the shade with time to linger over lunch and stories until the day's heat softens enough to cut pairs and head up the mountain.

Horses get watered in the creek and tied along the fence, dozing with heads hanging and cinches loose under their bellies. We splash cool water on our faces and hands and pull coolers from the pickups to the cottonwood shade by the stream. It's three o'clock and we're famished, but inside the coolers is every imaginable delight: tubs of fat roast beef sandwiches piled with lettuce, green pepper and red onion; Fritos, Cheetos, pretzels and salty potato chips; a gallon ice-cream bucket full of chilled and juicy cantaloupe, honeydew and watermelon; bags of Mary's homemade oatmeal chocolate-chip cookies; half-frozen jugs of iced tea and water. We fill our paper plates and pockets and find a spot of grass to spread out among friends and family, sure in the feeling that all of this—the food, rest and friendship—has been earned.

When we've eaten and drunk all that we've dreamed of through the long hot morning, I unzip my chaps and wad them for a pillow next to my husband and girls. Closing my eyes for a while, I listen to the cattle bawling out on the flats and the creek gurgling by my head and someone getting teased about a girlfriend or horse that outdid him or some other funny thing that might've happened ten years ago. After drifting off for maybe only a minute or two, I raise up and see that most everyone else is sprawled out, too, that I'm not the only one. And then, maybe about to doze off again, I hear that cow coming back toward the creek-crossing bawling for the calf she must think is back at Red Gulch. I hear Stan say to Mary, "I don't think I saw her calf all mornin', but her bag's not tight." And then Mary says, "He's here, that little baldy calf with the kink tail that lost his tag." Stan's spurs jangle as he stands up and throws a rock to turn the cow back. "Go on. You best go take another look; try a little harder." Then I hear those spurs jangling along the creek and kicking at a rock, making noise just to make noise, and I know that this time of resting is about over.

## SHELL CREEK

Crossing the empty highway below Granite Pass, I imagine myself stepping out into these currents of mountain air moving through hot, bright sun, the cattle bawling, my husband-to-be horseback on the slopes above us. It's late July, just days before the wedding, and my family's two vans have just rounded the long, slow curve out of the timber and pulled, one behind the other, into the turnout by the Antelope Butte ski area. The doors slide open, and crumpled, familiar bodies appear stretching and waving, the grandkids stumbling out around them and cameras already pointed at the riders on the slope above us. There are fourteen of them in all, come eighteen hundred miles for the wedding, camping cross-country with tents and coolers and sleeping bags.

"This crew's a wedding waiting to happen," my mother exclaims, embracing me.

My father follows with a hug and laugh. "Yes, all we need is one good shower and we're ready for anything!"

Both my sisters are here, one of my brothers, and three of the in-laws. I reach down to hug my nieces, all five of them, and my nephew, gathered around me rumpled and warm, showing me the rocks and feathers and treasures they've collected en route. I find myself entering a circle from which I've so long held myself apart. My family around me, come from so far and at such cost, I'm simply amazed and grateful. But then, this is what my family does. This is what my family can do.

On the slopes above us, Stan and Mary and Joe are pushing the cattle into new pasture and settling them onto the high benches of fresh grass above Granite Creek. Joe, his dark cowboy hat pulled low and silk scarf around his neck, sits his fine-boned liver chestnut, Poco. He turns and raises a hand in our direction.

"Is that the lucky guy?" my brother-in-law asks.

"Yep, that's the one. He promised me I could have as many horses as I wanted, so I said yes. Seems as good a reason as any, don't you think?" I point up the hill to where my sheepwagon's leveled in a clump of aspens. "We've got lunch up at the wagon, champagne in the spring, and coffee on the stove. Those guys'll be done soon."

From one of the vans, my father pulls out a cooler, and over his shoulder I can see my parents' silver service wrapped up in plastic and his black clerical robes and stole hanging from a hook. The whole back of the van's piled high with wedding presents, all wrapped in fancy pastels with white ribbons and cards tucked underneath.

"Dad, who on earth are all these from?"

"You'll see when we get them unloaded. They've been coming out of the woodwork the last few weeks, dropping these off. They'd all have come along if they could've."

I know where they've come from, of course; in my mind's eye I can see the gracious homes with perfect lawns and heirloom clocks ticking and chiming the hour inside, with season tickets to the symphony, church bulletins, leather-bound books, and generations of tradition. These are people who love my parents and so, without question, love me as well.

We walk back up the hill to my camp through a profusion of sticky purple geranium, bistort and forget-me-nots, hands full of children and cameras, Louise following on our heels. When Joe rides up to join us, he tips his hat and swings down off his horse in his spurs and batwing chaps with brass Texas stars down the sides, and I couldn't be more proud. He holds his reins in one hand and leans into hugs from everyone. With a smile spread across his face, he says, "Welcome to Wyoming," and holds me in his arms and kisses my hair as if he'd discovered gold.


Stan and Mary host a dinner that evening at their ranch house, with green chili enchiladas and salads, the good china brought out from the cupboards and our glasses clinking in toasts.

With the families combined, we overflow the dining table and scatter through the living room with plates on our laps.

I watch Joe across the table talking with my family, the smooth skin of his face nut-brown against his crisp white shirt, his back held straight and tall. Mostly quiet, he listens to their stories and nods, then cleans his wire-rimmed glasses on a napkin and takes a pull on a long-necked beer.

But in the course of the meal, his graciousness begins to unravel into stories I've heard countless times before, though my family hasn't, and I think that maybe he's still okay. I eye him nervously as his voice grows louder and louder.

After finishing dinner, we've gathered in the living room to open presents when the doorbell rings. It's my old boyfriend from Crystal Creek, stopping by to pick up fencing supplies he'd ordered from Stan and unaware of the occasion. He's greeted awkwardly at first but then, in the generous spirit of the evening, is invited in and given a plate and a beer. He finds an empty place on the rug next to Joe and flashes a grin around the room at us and the adventure he just stepped into. I watch closely as these unlikely friends sit and visit while the gifts are brought in and stacked around me. Though I try to catch Joe's eye, to call him to my side, he shies from the spotlight and sticks with Tom in the far corner, drinking in earnest now. My eyes scan the rambling log rooms to see if anyone has noticed, but if so they pretend they haven't. *Come kiss my hair. Come say you love me, that I'm your gold.* I open the presents one by one from family and friends, professors at the seminary in Lexington, members of the church in Nashville. My sisters are at my side jotting down notes and folding wrapping paper, and the pretty cards are passed around, and everyone's smiling so big. *If only it were just the two of us, it would be all right. I'd make it all right.* But he's too far across the room for me to bring him back. I pretend this is all somehow gallant, that it's how we do things out here, but when I look up again, they've tilted their heads together and are laughing at some little joke. And the next time I risk a glance, Joe has laid a big pink bow on top of his head and his eyes are drooping into a doze.

Curtis pulls his lemon yellow Cadillac convertible up to the back door of the Shell Community Hall and begins to unload coolers and boxes. Tall, thin and freckly with pale skin and coppery hair and glasses, he works for the Wyoming Highway Department but caters on the side and has agreed to do the food for our wedding. The day of the ceremony, he's ferrying everything from Basin, where he lives, the twenty-three miles to Shell. He's already made two trips and thought that would be that but then wanders over to the church, where Gretel is decorating, and decides his big red potted geraniums from home would look great on the bare white steps. So he races back to Basin, loads them up, and is driving ninety when the county deputy sheriff pulls him over. "He asked me if somebody was dyin', and I said, 'No, but Joe and Laura are about to get married and they need these geraniums.' And he said, 'Oh, well then. Slow it down. See you tonight!'" This, after all, is a man who'd bring us cold sodas on a cattle drive in his patrol car and flash his lights when we had to trail the cattle across the highway.

We marry early that evening in the Shell Community Church, a small white clapboard structure a block off the main street, next to the fire station and the log community hall. The date is July 27, 1983, a Wednesday evening, because it's the only day all my family can be with us before driving back across the country to their lives and jobs. "Give us the traditional," I'd said to my father, "the whole ball of wax." And when the vows are made and the kiss given, the tiny church comes to its feet in ovation, and hand in hand we nearly dance down the aisle and past the red potted geraniums to greet our friends outside under the leafy cottonwoods.

Coming out of the church into the bright sun, I kiss my new husband again and feel the smooth of his cheek against mine. He's wearing a linen suit and a pale-blue Western shirt and the silver squash-blossom belt buckle I'd given him as a wedding present. Behind us the celebrants empty onto the steps, spilling down through the bright geraniums and under the cottonwoods for shade, and for the first time I get to see who all has shown up from across the country and deep in my past.

John Hopkin has driven down from Montana with his partner, Charlie, and they're some of the first out the door. When the decision had been made to sell most of the sheep off the Lewis Ranch, John moved up to Billings to do maintenance work at the college and pursue a more liberal social life with the man who'd been an occasional visitor to his mountain cabin. "The work's a hell of a lot easier than sheep," he'd said with a laugh. "And sheepherders!" He's already smoking a ciga-rette, just steps away from the church, lifting his head and blowing smoke above the crowd as he leans to give me a hug. "Good thing you got outta the business. There ain't sheep one left on the outfit now." His gold ring flashes in the sun as he taps his ashes.

"I couldn't have done this without you, John."

"Hell, you know I never woulda missed it. And worth the trip just to see you all cleaned up."

Here are Butch and Charlene, a Nebraska couple who'd come with their horses to the northern Big Horns every fall just to hear the elk bugle, sharing meals, rides and stories with me and Grady and John. Dot and Mac from the church in Nashville, with whom my family had spent our first night when we arrived in 1960 to begin our life there; Dot has a small white rose with baby's breath pinned to her dress, part of the wedding party as she's volunteered to cut and serve the cake. My college friend, Gini, who'd flown in from Alaska with her father in his twin-engine plane, landing at the strip in Grey-bull, where I'd left a pickup for them to use. Jim and Beth in from Wisconsin with their week-old daughter, Moira. Jimmi and Burton, ranchers from the Sheridan side who I'd met while building fence along the elk refuge behind their place.

Gretel comes through the line with Press, who'd known Joe before his first marriage, back when he was cowboying for the Snake River Ranch and riding bulls at the county fair. They'd sung together in the bars around Jackson and on the Wind River Reservation, Press playing guitar and Joe singing in his clear, strong tenor with his head tipped back like a coyote, joy-ful, yodeling. Press had been his best man and known Amy as a baby. In my mind, I see the photograph of her mother, Linda, standing by a split-rail fence at the ranch they lived on in Morton, Wyoming, early in their marriage. She's holding Amy, only days old and bundled in a white blanket, with her eyes squinting into the sun and her hair pulled from her face in pigtails. There are freckles across her nose, and her mouth is turned into a shy smile, a tentative happiness. The photo has been trimmed with scissors to the size of Joe's wallet.

And then half of Shell Valley spills out behind, family and neighbors giving us hugs and congratulations and heading toward Shell Hall, where there's food and drink.

Missing are Amy, four at the time, and Jenny, eighteen months, tucked under the wings of Linda's family in Duluth with everyone still reeling from her death scarcely a year before. Joe's mother, Nadyne, has come from the Texas panhandle to stand for him in this marriage. Nate, as she's often called, is a retired English teacher, a petite woman of style and dash. She takes both of my hands in hers and leans close to whisper, "God must have sent you to Joe Ed. I was so afraid for my boy."

The log hall has been transformed with wildflowers and evergreen boughs brought down the mountain in the back of Joe's pickup the day before. My family had spent the day in the hall stringing lights, arranging tablecloths and filling vases with flowers, and when we enter, the white lights are twinkling and the buffet tables laden with sliced meats and cheeses and long fruit kabobs speared into half heads of purple cabbages that look to me like Sputniks.

The music begins with "Waltz Across Texas," and Joe leads me onto the dance floor for our first dance of the evening. He places a hand firmly on my lower back and mine goes to his shoulder. I feel his spine straighten and see his nostrils flare as he lifts his head slightly and begins to waltz me over the hardwood floor with sureness and grace as my long white skirt swirls around us and our friends clap and cheer.

By the next song, children and parents and grandparents are dancing with each other, with everyone, and spilling out through the doors to sit on straw bales and visit in the night air.

# HOME

On Christmas Eve, the first of my married life, I sit in the pew of a Lutheran church in Duluth at midnight Mass with the women of the family of my husband's first wife. It's their tradition to do this, without the men, after all the kids are tucked into bed. I have come into their family suddenly, and they've graciously moved over to make a place for me but at a cost I can't begin to imagine.

Before Christmas, Joe and I had worked for weeks on the girls' gift. We began with a large, sturdy cardboard box that we painted a bright magenta and collaged with magazine photos of dancers and princesses and cowgirls and pirates. Joe hinged the lid, and I glued a big mirror inside and surrounded it with sequins and glitter. Then we added the treasures we'd scoured from thrift stores and collected from friends: exotic hats and gloves, boots, flowered dresses and sequined shawls.

Jenny, barely two, pulls out her favorites and clomps through drifts of wrapping paper and ribbons in cowboy boots that come up to her thighs and a cowboy hat that falls over her eyes. Amy chooses a long purple silk dress, a strand of faux pearls and a wide-brimmed felt hat with a satin ribbon. She spins around in front of her aunt, flashing a quick five-year-old smile beneath the brim, and I can see that she will become a beautiful woman. As she stands for my camera, her skin is pale and her smile hesitant. How can she possibly know who or what I'm supposed to be to her? Even I have no idea of my place within this family, except that we're now bound by ties that will never disappear.

For the first several years of our marriage, we spend Christmas with the girls in Duluth, and they come west to be with us during the summers. Those mornings I leave early to drive up Shell Canyon to ride the Diamond Tail cattle in my care at Granite Pass and later up the same canyon to my job with the Big Horn National Forest. In my absence Joe braids the girls' long hair while they eat their breakfast, bleary eyed. Then he packs juice and snacks and loads them into the blue Chevy pickup, and together they make the morning rounds, shoeing horses around the valley and winning hearts along the way.

Evenings, I listen to them talk about kids they've met or a pool they've been invited to, cookies shared, stories told.

One summer my sister brings two of her daughters out to visit, and we pile everybody into the pickup and head up Shell Canyon. As Joe and I saddle the seven horses, Amy and Jenny drag blankets and bridles from the truck for us with an air of proprietary importance in front of our guests. We throw a pack saddle on an extra horse and fill the panniers with hotdogs and buns, ketchup, marshmallows, chips, apples, sunscreen, wildflower books and rain jackets. We pack up into the head of Salt Creek, all of us riding and some of the little ones doubled up, to check cattle and then build a campfire, roasting hotdogs and marshmallows on green branches we've whittled. Afterward, we sprawl full and warm around the fire, and I watch Amy and Jenny lean against their dad, owning him, the loud, bright hero of him, before their cousins.

"They need to be with you," I say that night in the dark. "You're their father, and they need to be with you."

I feel his body grow rigid, and he rolls over onto his back as if searching the sky through the ceiling. "I don't have the right. I gave that up when I took them to Duluth. I tried, but I just couldn't do it." I'd heard him confess how Jenny, only six months old, had been gathered up by her aunt and grandmother and flown from Texas back to Minnesota. Amy, three and a half years old, had seen her mother fall from her horse, seen her limp body, heard the ambulance's sirens. Joe had held on to her, trying to keep her in Texas, where as a toddler she spent long hours bundled up in the saddle with him or in the tractor cab with her arms flung around his neck. But her tears wouldn't stop, and she was afraid to be alone, following him from room to room and wanting only to be in his arms. Finally, facing down his shortcomings, he'd moved with her to Duluth so she could be encircled by the constant and loving women of her family. He'd tried making a living cutting timber, but for him it had been a winter of grief in all its destructive guises.

"But this isn't about you," I say. "It's about *them*. You're their father, and they need to be with you."


The seed is planted, and when I'm offered a seasonal job with the Big Horn National Forest, administering their public grazing lands, I take it. My reluctance to leave the Diamond Tail is tempered by the possibility of a permanent job with health insurance and benefits for our family. The country I ride now expands from the Granite allotment to include Shell Creek, Medicine Lodge, Paintrock Creek and the Cloud Peak Wilderness. We buy the six acres on Beaver Creek and a house that needs a lot of work. Winter nights I spend worrying over garden catalogues and plotting my orders, wandering around the property by daylight trying to imagine it populated with the lush color and abundance promised by those pages.


Packages begin arriving in the mail, seedlings of cottonless cottonwood, Nanking cherry, wild plum, chokecherry, crabapple, green ash, weeping red birch, golden willow and weeping willow. I unwrap the bundles and place them in buckets of water and begin digging holes into the dark of evening. I hook up the horse trailer and drive to a nursery sixty miles away to buy six

Colorado blue spruce trees that are already four feet tall, imagining the day when they'll form a solid green windbreak to the north of the house, as well as three green ash trees, two inches in diameter, that would become tall and sprawling, shading us from the harsh western light of summer. For the big trees I dig big holes. I walk the yard for hours and stand dreaming in one spot or another. I decide the spruce trees are too close together and I replant the whole line of them. I carry a shovel along to my forest service job and at the end of the day dig up small clumps of aspen shoots, wild blue flax, wild rose and yellow shrubby cinquefoil, sneaking them down the mountain and putting them into the holes I had waiting, packing them back in the ground with peat and manure and Miracle-Gro, then giving them a good soak often after the sun has set. I bring home buckets of daffodils, irises and day lilies that friends have divided from their gardens and dig holes for them, as well, along the fence rows, among the cottonwood seedlings by the creek and flanking the west side of the house.

One day Joe pulls up with three sandstone slabs he'd found in the hills and manhandled up into the bed of his truck. "There's more," he said, "enough that if we hunt around a little we could do the front of the house like we talked." Later he unloads railroad ties at the front door, starts his chainsaw and creates containment walls for the sand and stone. We make trip after trip into the hills to scout for rock, pushing the limits of what we can lift, and the terrace grows and slowly takes shape.

When school lets out, the girls come to stay with us. Jenny's five this summer, with olive skin and shadowy eyes, her hair pulled back in tight braids. Amy's eight, her fair skin pinked at her cheeks with sun, her long hair sunbleached and braided. On her very first visit I'd courted her with her favorite, macaroni and cheese, buying expensive Emmenthaler and Gruyère and stirring heavy cream and nutmeg into it. She'd pushed it around her plate, trying to be polite, but finally admitted she really preferred the kind from the box, "but the salad's very good." And so I learned to buy her mac and cheese in a box and white bread rather than wheat and to not add dill to tomato soup or pepper to eggs. There were standards, though, that I felt I had to uphold, certain things a mother should do, and one night, edgy and tired, I'd told Jenny, "One brussel sprout. Just one. It won't hurt you to try something new for a change. You're not leaving this table until you do." She speared one with great difficulty and got it into her mouth, whole, and when I looked back, her eyes were wide and welling with tears, fixed on her plate, the awful thing too big to chew or swallow. "Oh, Jenny. God, I'm sorry. Just spit it out. You tried." Then she opened her mouth, let it drop to the plate and began to cry in earnest.

Our first garden grows up rich and lush, the vegetables huge in this virgin creek-bottom soil. The kids carve zucchini boats and sail them down the creek, play softball with zucchini bats while I hover over everything in a frenzy, building a house, scrubbing it clean, working my job, keeping my husband's edges tucked in, protecting the idea of our marriage, smiling while simmering below. I weed and pick and cook and freeze furiously after work and on the weekends, believing that a life can be built by hard work and a home created by sheer force.

I am wrong, as it turns out, but I do the best I can.

. . .

That first summer at Beaver Creek, Hannah comes to live with us, the sixteen-year-old daughter of the Swedish man who'd been our exchange student when I was a young teen. She arrives with her parents and brother and, enchanted with the west, stays on for nearly two months to help take care of the girls in exchange for a chance to ride. She's tall, blonde, and sweet tempered, and the girls idolize her as a big, worldly sister. The days are hot, so we pull mattresses and bedding out for all of them on the front porch, where banks of shuttered windows open to the creek bottom and hayfields and the big windows on either end let the night breezes through. Late one night, waking to thunder and lightning, I leave my bed and pad toward the porch and hear Hannah and Amy whispering, giggling, then see the light of flashlights and their books, their blonde heads nearly touching. Jenny is fast asleep beside them, her legs bare and chubby still. "Are you guys okay? Is the rain blowing in?" There's a flash of light, a deep rumble that shakes the earth. I sit down and linger in their sisterly companionship, reluctant to return to my silent bed.

Joe brings me coffee in bed every morning in the dark, shaking my shoulder gently and saying, "Okay, it's ready; it's time." I've heard him rustling around in the kitchen and stoking the fire in the woodstove in the living room, letting the dogs out, knowing that I could stay under the covers a little longer, safe, warm, cared for. He sets the coffee cups on the side table and props the pillows up behind me, climbing in next to me and handing over a mug of black coffee that steams in a room where frost creeps up the northern wall in the winter. We sip coffee in the early dark, without speaking, and watch the windows for signs of dawn. It is in this hour that we find our comfort, that we can believe each day is fresh, that the hurts from the day before have been erased, that saying we love each other is enough.

The sagging porch of Press and Gretel's old gypsum-block house wraps around two sides and looks over the distant pond to where the horizon drops off into the basin. This late-summer evening we're saying farewell to our friends Sonia and Robert, who are leaving Shell and heading for the northwest coast. "A change of pace," she'd said in explanation. "Better jobs and the ocean." When we arrive, Gretel has draped an ivory damask tablecloth over the old picnic table out in the grass, amid scattered dog bones and cowpies. She's coming out of the house headlong in a flannel shirt, her arms wrapped around a tarnished silver champagne bucket filled with ice and a bottle of something French. "This is a dreadful affair," she says, "so we may as well spruce things up a little." Press and Joe grill brook trout over an open fire for hors d'oeuvres while Amy, Jenny and I set the table with silver, linen napkins and their best crystal. Gretel finds a few blooms that the deer haven't eaten and arranges them in a low vase just as Sonia and Robert pull up. She gets out and comes across the yard, opening her arms, saying, "Shall we just drink and cry all night?" We start with champagne and move to red wine as the light slants and steaks and roasting corn come off the grill. We peel the papery husks back and toast one another across the table with the ears, and when we're done, we toss the cobs over our shoulders into the grass and gathering dusk. We laugh and laugh, but I can feel the tears lining up for our loss. I can't imagine my life without them, without Sonia listening patiently to the sorrows of my marriage. I don't yet know this is just the first crack in this small community, that other friends around this table will follow in the next years, that I will have to turn to my husband to be my friend.

"You own your own home and you want more? Think of all the people in the world who don't have this. Can't you just be happy the way things are?" These days it seems I'm always proposing something—small things, a trip with the girls, a class together, or the same big thing, for him to quit drinking. More than anything I just want him to talk to me, to show up, to be with me. With some of my closest friends now gone, I push hard until one day he erupts in anger. "You want too damn much from me. You want to talk; go talk to someone else. You want to make love; go make love to someone else. This is all I've got."

We're on the couch in the living room, but he stands to say this and leans over in my face, so I feel as small and powerless as a child. Once my tears have dried, I make it my mission to take him at his word. In my travels I look for the glance, the opening to have an affair, and tell him about my plans. He nods his head calmly, supportively, and arranges to pick up the kids while I'm off in another town meeting a man for whom I feel no joy. When his face remains smooth and calm, I push the knife in deeper; when he still doesn't seem to feel it, I use both hands and twist hard at his guts until he does. One night I find him waiting for me on the flagstone terrace in front of the house, and he clutches my collar in rage and swings me from side to side, saying words that are more like explosions. I disappear, limp in his hold, and look down for sharp things that might hurt me if he were to throw me down, though I never really believe that he will. I am quiet and soft in his grasp, not meeting his eyes, but some part of me feels a rush of relief. *Here you are, the man I knew was inside. Here you are, angry behind that smooth face.* After he's worn himself out, he comes to a stop, panting, still clutching my collar, yet I still don't look up into his eyes, just at the ground, saying nothing. His breath is heavy at my ear with the sour smell of alcohol and then the raspy gravel of tears held back for years, long before me, long before the loss of his first wife, held back now, too, but coming anyway. It is black night and the crickets drone. I can hear Beaver Creek gurgling in the willows below the house. Joe quietly loosens his grip and stands crying with his head bent low. I look up into the dark silhouette of his face but can't see his eyes, only the stars above his head. I hold myself next to the black shape of him for one long moment, unable to step into that opening of grief, maybe too long in coming, or maybe my heart grown too hard. After a brief hesitation, I slip away in the dark to my car and drive away.

When it comes down to it, he chooses alcohol. "This is who I am," he tells me. "Take me or leave me. I don't want to read the books or go to a shrink or sit in a circle and talk about it." He says this without malice, with an elemental sureness, like a holy man revealing an inner truth. Six months later he hooks up the horse trailer and helps me move my belongings to town.

. . .

In February I go to Kentucky to visit my parents, waiting for my divorce to be final. On a Sunday morning following the church service downtown, I'm in the kitchen with my mother. "I feel like you're ashamed of me," I say as she scrapes out a pot at the stove, her back to me.

When she finally turns around, her jaw is clinched and it looks as if she may cry. "All I've ever heard from you was how perfect your marriage was. How could you not know he was an alcoholic when you married him? You made your bed and you should lie in it. You don't just quit because it's not working." She turns back to the stove and says to the wall, "I can't bear to see my children get divorced."

The blood drains from my head and face, the tears gather at my eyes. There are no words for me to say. I understand that much of what she says is true. I have always shared with her the joy, the adventure, the winning stories I could tell from eighteen hundred miles away. I never, ever shared with her the suffering, barely knew how to speak the words to myself.

I go to her and place my hands on her shoulders and slowly turn her around and put my arms around her. She feels thin, even brittle, beneath my arms, a slim reed determined not to break. I am her second child to divorce, and I understand that it destroys something in her, but I'm drowning and cannot help.


I wait to hear her leave for work the next morning, then find my slippers. My father has the fireplace going in the den and coffee waiting for me. In his retirement, he's been making trips to the Soviet Union to visit Russian Orthodox churches and taking classes in language, liturgy and now literature at the university.

He's seated at the card table with his Tolstoy and Dostoyevsky scattered around him, his reading glasses perched on his nose. "Good morning, sunshine," he says, pouring the coffee.

"Good morning, Dad."

"How are you this morning?"

"Okay," I settle on the couch with my cup and pull a blanket over my legs. Then, almost an afterthought: "I guess I've been better."

My father watches me, silent for a long time. "This is hard for her. You know she loves you."

"I do," I say. "I know she does."


The following morning I go with her to work. Helping Hands is a day-center for people suffering from Alzheimer's, one she conceived and spearheaded. While her father was being ravaged by the disease, she'd gone back to school, gotten her master's degree in social work, and was hired by the Sanders-Brown Center on Aging, where she developed a program based on the concept that each person with Alzheimer's should have a "best friend," a volunteer who knows their history, can aid their memory and acknowledge them, helping them feel safe and cared for.

She leans over to greet an elderly woman who's sitting at a table. She hugs her, then takes hold of her hand. "Rose," she says, "I want to introduce my daughter to you. This is Laura.

She's a cowgirl out West. Isn't that something? Rose has three daughters of her own—don't you, Rose? They take such good care of you and must have given you this pretty sweater. Aren't we proud of our daughters?"

Rose is smiling, beaming with love for her daughters.

"Rose, Laura's going to be your best friend this morning. Laura, Rose will show you her favorite book, which has pictures of the town where she grew up."

When I sit down next to Rose, she takes my hand and smiles into my eyes. "It's very good to see you again," she whispers, her social graces intact even if her memory is not.

We page through her book looking at the pictures, and she occasionally points at one and smiles at me as though it's a memory we share, and I squeeze her hand and smile back, even though my heart's in my throat.

I watch my mother make the rounds of all the tables, lingering over every one after a kiss on the cheek, her gaze full and open and adoring as she takes their hands in hers and their faces light with joy. I can't take my eyes away from her, this person I've never seen, my mother, this stranger, and I feel tears gathering for want of her. I long to be the one in her gaze, in her arms, for her to love me as she loves these people who haven't disappointed her, who haven't let her down, whose messy lives are not her burden. I blink my eyes and wipe my tears and wish myself in a place far, far away from this mirror of my longing, in a place where I am all that I need.

## LEAVING

In the night I wake to the sound of something that has just happened and cannot name it. In the moments that follow, my eyes open to the dark and I struggle to place myself, the bed, the room, the life I'm sunk into. A man's voice coming through the wall. Something falling to the floor and shattering, glass. Laughter, dark and hollow. The hands on my bedside clock say 2:15. My eyes adjust and I see light seeping through the blinds from the street and make out the door to the bathroom, the door into the kitchen. Salt Lake, then, is where I am, and the pieces of my life stack back into a pile that has shape and form.

There are no children sleeping upstairs, no horses in the shed, only my drunken recluse of a neighbor in the other half of this small bungalow duplex. I fall back into the covers and pull them up tight around me. Through the gap in the blinds, I watch the snow falling in swaths of light, constant and heavy, and search my mind for someone or something I should worry for in the storm, but there is no one, nothing. It seems a distant memory, breaking open bales of bright, clean straw and kicking it loose, charging through it like a kid in a puddle, to make deep piles from wall to wall in the tiny shed for a sick calf with droopy ears. Or on the winter feedground, with the skies falling dark around us, a gate thrown open to willow bottoms and the cattle stringing through it to tall grass, dried and rattling, that can rise up around the night's slick calves like nests from the wind. Under the covers my hands grip each other, and I feel their hard, blunt strength. *This is who I am. This is what I can do.* I think of the girls breathing their dreams in and out from under soft down while the ice froze thick and vast and the world conspired for us a trail both treacherous and sublime. *How are we to know?* The question rises into the dark and hangs, a presence lingering over my wakefulness. *How are we to know? These hands hovered over you and kept you warm, but it was never enough, not ever, and now I'm far and cannot do even that.*


The Cliff Lodge sits at an elevation of nine thousand feet up in Little Cottonwood Canyon, just below Alta at the wide-open head of the valley. The road that winds up there is known to be the most avalanche-prone road of any in the lower forty-eight states. Some nights it closes in the heavy snows, and I camp in the spa, sleeping on my massage table.

One whole wall of the small room where I work on the ninth floor is glass, and I can look out into the top branches of Engelmann spruce and the steep mountain slopes beyond. I begin work at three in the afternoon and, when fully booked, do six sessions in as many hours. People arrive in robes, and leave in robes and while I work on them, the light gathers into alpenglow and dims to dusk, and the ski patrol makes last sweeps of the mountain. When it snows, I feel as though I'm working inside a Christmas snow globe, the flakes swirling around my head.

Two years after the divorce, I had rented a small storage space near the railroad tracks in Greybull and given away to friends anything that wouldn't fit—bed frame, mattress, ironing board, charcoal grill. I left behind me a kind man, my two girls, and a permanent position with the forest service I'd always thought I wanted. Then, with car loaded, I drove south to Salt Lake to study massage. I wanted to ride the pendulum of experience in the opposite direction and to see who I might be if I left the country of my failures behind.

When the light begins to slant across the slopes, I prepare myself for work, bundling my clothes under the cupboard and pulling on black pants, a white shirt and an apron that ties around my waist, then clip my hair back, scrub my nails and wait for my first client. They arrive exhausted and elated from steep slopes and deep powder, from days spent in the thin air of altitude. Behind them in their lives they have left jobs, schedules, pressure. Behind them in their lockers they have left rings, diamonds, cell phones, designer clothes. They come to me naked and wrapped in a plain white robe, bringing with them only what is left—hope, regret or reflection. They crawl onto my table, compliant and empty, often leaving even their voices behind.

Silence. I know this territory like the back of my hand and can take people there. The world breathes in and breathes out; the wind shifts and stills. In my mind I'm under the night sky of solitude, immense and comforting in its shelter, the smell of sage a balm. It feels a risk to go there, but people follow me into this space and then they come back.

One night I work on a woman who is a neonatal cardiologist. It's a wrap, not a massage, so I lead her into a dimly lit room lined with cedar and redwood. After she showers and scrubs, I wrap her in steaming hot towels and linens that have been steeped in an herbal brew of lavender and chamomile. She looks like a mummy lying there on her back on the table with an outer layer of heavy wool blanket that leaves only her face and the top of her head exposed. I wring washcloths from a bucket of ice water at my feet and apply them to her face and the base of her neck as she sweats in her cocoon. I massage her scalp. I offer water through a straw and lean over her to apply compression to her shoulders, sternum, hip bones, knees and ankles to remind her that her body's still there. I part the blanket at her feet and massage them with cool hands, then sit on the bench by her head in the near dark and complete silence. I hold my hands on either side of her head, sometimes shifting to put one on her crown and the other on her forehead. I pray for her silently, though I don't know exactly what that means, only that this is the one place in my life where I can be unflinchingly tender.

The woman has been quiet but now begins to cry. "I work every day on tiny babies, on their hearts: I open them up. Every day I am responsible for so much. I'm sorry. I never expected this." And then she's quiet again.

Through the years, I work on many clients who ski several different weeks at Snowbird each season. They return six nights in a row, then once more in the spring and the same again the following years. I work on their spouses and friends and occasionally their children. Sessions are mostly spent in silence. I seldom speak except to ask about an injury or the pressure, but sometimes people want to talk. If they're too chatty, I ask them to take a deep breath and then another to shut them up, though often what comes out is soulful and engaging.

One night the client's a man I've worked on several years running. I ask how his year has been, and this otherwise delicate man says simply, "It sucked."

"Excuse me?"

"It sucked," he says again and explains that his wife had left him and then returned in the course of a torturous year. He asks how mine has been, and I flush immediately to tears, but he can't see. "Is there someone special in your life?"

"No."

After a long pause, he says, "I can't believe that you don't have a man in your life who wouldn't leap at the chance to move heaven and earth for you."

I ask him to take a deep breath and then another, and I keep on working.

My work is deep and slow, and after a few minutes he sinks into a quiet place, and all I can hear is the sound of his breathing. Early on I'd learned to drop my table low and lean my weight into it, stripping between the muscles to loosen them and using pressure points to release energy. Near the end of the session I rub his scalp vigorously to bring him back and then close my hands over the top of his skull, over his ears, my fingers tingling and sparking. I pull them ever so slightly away and imagine his skull expanding with my hands to make a bigger space inside. I imagine a flock of wild blackbirds rising in a spiral out of this space, up through my hands and arms and up out of the top of my own head, into the air above us.

Driving southwest out of Salt Lake, I head toward the small Mormon town of Tooele, pronounced "too-will-ah." On the pickup seat next to me is the newspaper with an ad circled: *Blue merle Australian shepherd female, six months, $250.* I've never paid money for a dog and don't intend to today, though I've been to all the pounds without finding a match. Next to the newspaper is a framed photograph of my old sheepdog, Louise, a head shot that captures her blue eye and imperious nature as she lords her position on top of the hay wagon over Handy, the ranch dog, trotting along on the road below. Louise was born in the winter of 1977 in a bed scratched out under a low-hanging evergreen in the town of Cowley. She herded sheep, punched cows on the Diamond Tail, and followed me horseback through my years with the forest service. By the time I divorced in

1992, she'd grown deaf and blind, wandering around the Beaver Creek house and yard by memory and feel. Knowing she couldn't make the transition and that Joe would care for her better than anyone in the world, I entrusted her to him for the end of her days. One morning he called in tears to say he'd found her dead, curled up in her bed on the back porch and facing a mountain that she couldn't see.

When I pull into the address from the ad, I find a neatly appointed double-wide with thick shrubbery and well-tended flowerbeds. Bird feeders hang from every tree. Irises and daffodils bloom profusely. When no one answers my knock, I start toward the barn and here comes a man with a dog over the small bridge that crosses the creek. She keeps close to his boots, stepping gingerly and checking his face as though ready to run to me but knowing she shouldn't. The man is tall, thin and dark with a shock of gray hair. "Go ahead," he says. "It's okay." And she races up to me and sits at my feet, looking up into my face with her blue and brown and yellow eyes, and there's a crazy little snip of black running down her nose, and I know that of course I have come to take her home. Of course I have.

"I'd be really good to her. I've had an Australian shepherd before," I say, turning the photograph of Louise over to show him.

"I've no doubt you two would get along famously."

"She'll have a good life. We're headed back to Wyoming this summer, and she'll have nothing but space, and we'll be together every day." I notice that his eyes are crinkled in amusement, but I can't help myself and add, "I'm very responsible."

"I've already said yes," he laughs.

I realize that I don't need to talk him into this. "Are you sure you can part with her?"

"To a good home, yes."

I write him a check, and he walks with me back to my pickup. I open my door, uncertain as to how she'll leave this man and the home she's known, but when he says, "Load up," she leaps inside. As I drive away, she sidles over against me and leans her weight into my shoulder, her front legs braced on the seat and her eyes, inches from mine, watching the road alongside me

I wake early one Sunday morning when the spring snows are melting, make a thermos of coffee and a ham and cheese sandwich, and then drive east out of Salt Lake along Interstate 80. Grace is perched in the passenger seat with her head slightly ducked under the visor, studying the road and the country intently. I mean to drive to the Wyoming state line to sit and read for a while and have my coffee, but once there I find it isn't far enough. I keep going, past Evanston, nearly a hundred miles in all, to the exit for Highway 189. Here there are no gas stations, no services of any kind, only a narrow two-lane road that heads north into the sagebrush toward the town of Kemmerer and the spring sheep ranges along the way. I pull over and park behind a gravel pile and turn the pickup off. It's April and the meadowlarks are singing. Grace follows me out into the sage, where we squat and pee, and then follows me back. Propped against the wheel, I pour coffee and split a ham sandwich between us. She licks her lips and lays her head on my knees and stares deeply into my eyes, hoping for more. I read the morning through, enduring her devotion, and when the sun rises high in the sky and the air has warmed, I wad my jacket beneath my head and sprawl on the ground, sleeping the long, deep sleep of the protected.

# THE STONE SCHOOL

---

In early May the Wyoming air holds a thin warmth that won't survive the falling light. Returning for the summer, I pull the pickup off the empty Shell highway onto the gravel drive and stop to open the pole gate of the old Stone School. The sun hangs over the horizon and evening light casts long-branched shadows through the brush and coppers the rough-hewn limestone of this solitary building. From a nearby fence post, a meadowlark calls out its complicated flute notes. The hinges screech, and prairie dogs scatter to ground, popping back up to watch from a distance. I leave the gate propped open on a pine stump and drive into the yard of what will be my home for the next six months.

For many years I have passed it by, driving the highway between Greybull and Shell. It has always seemed lonesome and stark, but in 1903, with kids arriving horseback and afoot from the scattered farmsteads, it would have been the center, the logical place to build a one-room schoolhouse. The limestone blocks had been quarried from the eastern flanks of the Big Horns to form a room roughly twenty by forty feet, with solid wood double doors opening south to the road and a bell tower rising from the cedar-shaked roof. On either of the long sides to the east and west are three tall, deep-silled windows. To the north, looking out over the cottonwood bottoms of Shell Creek, there had once been only a small door that opened to the outhouse, the woodpile, and the bluff's edge.

My friend John McGough—nicknamed Roadkill for his penchant to retrieve and recycle dead animals along the highway—bought it in 1980 after years of vacancy and disrepair. He later engaged an architect to design an addition in the rear—including a cathedral-ceilinged living area, small sleeping loft, and an office with an oak spiral staircase—that maintained the roof line and the integrity of the old school. The tall windows continue around the new addition, and French doors open onto the deck that wraps around the east side toward the mountains. He replaced the solid front doors with tall glass ones that let in the southern light.

At the back door, I find a big rock holding down a note from Amy and Jenny: *Welcome home, Chica. We'll be by after play practice.* I open the double doors and on the table see a potted red begonia blooming with a note from John: *Some-*

*thing for your new camp.* I wander through to the big front room, lit gold by the day's last light. For the last few summers, the school has served as a bookstore and gallery for the locals and tourists en route to Yellowstone, and this year I'm here to manage it. The walls are hung with photographs of native rock art and scattered oils and Western prints. In the deep windowsills are collections of fossils, bones and shells, with rattlesnake skins curled and draped among them. Pine bookcases line the walls of the southeastern corner, and in the fading light I see shelf after shelf of Western history, natural history, geology and literature. The room smells of warm cedar, pine and woodsmoke from the cast-iron stove in the back.

From the deck, I pick out the landmarks from south to north, where the range disappears into the northern dusk. Trapper Creek, White Creek, Shell Creek, the two forks of Horse Creek, Beaver Creek, Pete's Hole, Five Springs. This is the bare mountain face I have stared at for most of my adult life, and naming each canyon, I know that I have walked and ridden and trailed livestock up them all, in this place I know, that is in my blood.

Quick as that, it goes dark and the air chills. I turn on the lights, give the back rooms a good sweeping and begin to unload the pickup, starting with my sleeping bag and coffee makings for morning. Then the few treasures I carry with me in this pared-down version of my life. Amy's clay horse sculpture from fifth-grade art class. A watercolor of desert cactus and stars from the girls' aunt Mary. The improbable and cumbersome love seat with the big pillows from my marriage. I leave the French doors open to the evening and the girls' arrival, though the air is cool.

It's after nine when I hear their car on the gravel drive and see headlights swinging through the dark. I step out on the deck to meet them with my heart in my throat, and then they're out of the car and into the swath of light from inside. Amy is seventeen, a senior, her blonde hair long around her face and her eyes wide-open windows like her mother's. Jenny is fourteen and gangly, in that awkward stage of braces and baggy flannel shirts, not quite grown into her beauty. Together, they're two shades of the same color as they move through the porch light and into my arms. I'd seen them only occasionally since leaving my forest service job and moving from Greybull a year and a half before, and our phone conversations had sometimes been a game of twenty questions without many answers. While waiting for them, I had imagined hesitation and reserve, but here they are laughing, delighted, and in this moment I'm only grateful that they have welcomed back the one who left.

"Come in, come in. Tell me everything you know." I make us tea and pull out biscotti and good chocolate brought up from the city. The school play is *Anne of Green Gables,* and Amy has the part of Anne's bosom buddy, Diana.

"Can you come to rehearsal?"

"Of course."

"Tomorrow?"

"Yes."

"And Jenny's track meet's on Friday."

"Okay, I'll be there. Shall we do dinner here, after?"

"Let's make homemade pizzas again."

In an hour we've concocted a social calendar for the next weeks and planned the brunch I'd promised Amy to celebrate her high school graduation in the open, sunlit great room of the Stone School.


The storm moved in quietly during the night and dropped a soft, soaking rain, a rarity in this high-desert country that sees mostly wind and lightning. What remains at dawn are the softly torn edges of clouds lodged along the mountain's rock face and clinging in thin streamers to the bare landscape of the basin. The air is charred with the smell of wet sage and the neighbor's ditch fire gone wild into the greasewood thicket. Tendrils of moisture rise up and take on the color of morning light.

From my bed, I heard the cries of sandhill cranes coming close and loud through the east window of the second-floor loft. Peering through binoculars, I found them, a pair, under a cottonwood across the hay meadow east of the schoolhouse with the sun rising behind them and their cries becoming more agitated. As I scanned the area, my heart jumped to see a red fox sitting on his haunches just a few yards away with his nose aimed at them, his tail curled around him. The cranes were leaning toward him with their wings lifted, imposing, shifting their weight from leg to leg, and it was unclear to me who was doing the harassing. But then the cranes stepped forward with wings still raised, and the fox gave up his position, turning to sniff at the hay stubble and saunter off.

From this alcove, I have a perfect view, so I return later in the morning to look for the cranes. What I see instead are foxes, two adults and four kits gamboling about under the cottonwood. So, this is their den, which the fox had been defending against the cranes. The sun rises higher, and the kits disappear until later in the day, but I go obsessively to the window with binoculars to watch.

What my life is again: horses, saddles, space, massage, words that will eventually come out, light that won't quit, birdsong in the early morning. Friends stop by with food and flowers. The girls drop by daily, coming and going from town to their father's house. There are school plays, awards nights, dinners with a breeze sifting in through the French doors. Geese fly in strings along the creek bottom, and wild blue flax opens in fragile, cheerful waves out the back door.

Gathering cattle one morning out of the Sulphur pasture with Stan and Mary and their crew, he sends me off with their daughter Carol to the far hinterlands after a small bunch their neighbor had spotted from the plane. Carol is tall and lanky, with short dark hair and the fair skin and freckles of her Irish ancestors. In the years that I worked for her family on the ranch, we became friends in our own right. Through this friendship and her connection with my Kentucky family, she met my brother and eventually married him. After living in Kentucky and studying there with Wendell Berry, she led my brother back west, to Cody, and my family grew in numbers around me.

We head off at a steady trot, slowing to climb the ridges, one after another, according to the vague instructions we'd been given. Nearly an hour later we spot the little cluster of renegades, tucked along a wet seep in the bottom of a draw, and slide our horses down off the soft ridge to get behind them and worry them down the narrow trail. Each draw opens into another, and we have no choice but to follow them down from one to the next, the ridges rising above us to block our view and sense of direction until we finally spill out into a broad basin ringed by cliffs.

"Where the hell are we?"

"Beats me."

"But didn't you ride this country? Didn't you *live* out here?"

"It's been ten years. And this just doesn't make sense to me. Maybe we came off the allotment at that last gate."

"Maybe."

"Do you think we're in the wrong place?"

She turns in her saddle and grins. "You know what Dad says. If you've got cattle, you're always in the right place."

We scan the horizon and spot a horse and rider atop one ridge, as though they've been watching for us. We take it as a sign and begin working our tired bunch in their direction.

"That's Dad."

"How on earth can you tell from here?"

"If it were Mom, she'd be bailing off the ridge to help us, and he's just sitting there watching. Nope, that's Dad."

As we get closer, he finally guides his horse down the ridge alongside us. "You still remember all these plants?"

"Some."

"What's this?"

"Slender wheatgrass."

"This?"

"Needle and thread." I lean over my saddle and point out

bottlebrush squirreltail, Indian ricegrass, Great Basin wildrye, prince's plume, mariposa lily, copper mallow, Indian pipe. We plod along behind the balky cattle, the sun rising higher in the sky and turning up the heat.

"Well," he says, "I'm glad to see you haven't lost all your good sense down there in Utah."

I scan the meadow to the east for the foxes and find them at their den. The mother stands patiently while the kits suckle her, bumping into her and one another in their hunger until she races off to the south about fifty yards and flattens herself behind a tall clump of grass. Thinking she's seen a predator and taken cover, I swing my binoculars back on the kits, but they're bouncing through the grass like popcorn, their white-tipped tails like flags in the sage. They find their mother, and she leaps up, exploding them into the air again, and with them on her heels she chases around for the sheer fun of it. A pickup truck drives slowly down the lane behind them. The willows are thin cover, and I'm afraid for them, so exposed.

The basement under the addition is set deep into the ground with high ceilings and unshakable walls. I prepare a room for massage and place an ad in the paper and wait to see what happens, but they come. One elderly man has his wife sit with him during the session and chews snoose, keeping his spit cup within reach the whole time. A woman in her eighties with no family for thousands of miles comes weekly. A butcher tells me, "I'm tired of killing." A schoolteacher grieves for her lost daughter. A cowboy thrown from a horse hobbles in. One night, late, the phone rings and a drunken voice asks if I work late, and there's a chorus of laughter in the background. The phone rings and rings until I unplug it.

Late that summer Tim is diagnosed with lymphoma. The silent, often aloof member of a family otherwise prone to speak their minds, he becomes an awkward center. When he begins chemotherapy, I offer somewhat hesitantly to give him a massage every week as a gift; such tenderness feels risky in this cowboy world of mine, and especially with Tim, as stoic as they come. But he says yes, gladly, and shows up week after week in varying stages of pain, weakness and exhaustion. Often he arrives straight off the tractor, smelling of diesel, with orange baling twine and cattle syringes spilling from his pockets. The first session is one of sympathy and sadness, and afterward he seems drugged, almost in a stupor. In the weeks that follow I focus on his energy, resting a hand on his head and the other on his sacrum, gathering up energy and willing it to move through his spine. It sounds silly, and it takes courage. I'm not sure I know what I'm doing, but it can't hurt. He comes out lightened and refreshed.

"My legs have been the worst," he says. "Weak. Won't always hold me up."

"Maybe you're learning that you don't always have to stand on your own two feet. Sometimes you can ask for help."

"Ain't that the truth."

. . .

I go to see Mary, who's waiting the day out for Tim's test results after the chemo. "I think the waiting's the worst part of it all," she says and pours me a cup of tea. She tells me about Carol's trip to Rome and that she and my brother had visited the Pantheon, which Mary explains is the world's largest unsupported dome and has a hole in the top. Her voice is quivering, and I wonder where she's headed with this. "When it rains and there are people inside," she says, "they close all the outside doors, and the heat from their bodies rises up through the hole and keeps out the rain." She pauses. "I feel like if we all just hold hands around Tim, we can keep the harm away."

Through that summer and fall, I work on him. I work on his parents and his brother and sisters and aunts and uncles and an ever-expanding circle of friends and family to which he has become a center.


The wind howls all through the night and brings snow in the early morning hours and then moves on. I lean out the window and listen to the stillness. The world is spare, flat, covered in hoarfrost, the mountains invisible in an icy fog. One fox circles the outer edges of the meadow, hunting, but I scan the den and ditches and silvered willows and see nothing else moving. Before the winds, there'd been shots, and through the window I'd seen a spotlight sweeping the field. I'm glad I'm not a fox today. They have no safe place.


I coax Jenny into staying with me for a week, and she unpacks her things in neat piles in the drawers I've cleared for her. We share the bed upstairs as it's the only one, watching movies and drinking hot chocolate there in the evenings, coffee in the mornings. Fresh out of the shower, her hair all slicked away from her face, her eyes deep lidded and shadowed in her olive skin, she laughs shyly, hiding her braces, but I glimpse the woman she will become. We plant a few seeds in the raised beds out back: lettuce, onions, carrots, squash. When the nights warm, friends gather on the deck, and we make home-made pizzas and snip blooms from the wildflower garden for the table.

As a child she had always followed me around asking about the names of flowers and trees, and these seemed the easiest of lessons to impart. When my parents came out one Thanksgiving, my mother brought her a book that identified animal tracks, and we went out under a full moon and crunched through the snow down by the creek with the book and a flashlight, exploring the movements of raccoons and rabbits. In second grade she'd been designated her class's "star of the week" and needed to answer questions about herself for a big class poster, and she worried over her answers nearly to the point of tears.

"I don't know what I want to be when I grow up. I love too many things. Maybe science, I could be a scientist. But I like art and music, and I might want to be an artist. Or maybe a nurse like my mom?" She looked up at me for guidance.

"How about putting down 'renaissance woman' as your answer? That means you're broadly interested in both the arts and sciences, a woman of vast accomplishment."

Her face had lit up with this solution. "How do you spell that?"

John McGough shows up one morning with the old wood-fired hot tub in the back of his pickup. "I thought you might have more use for this here," he says, "than I would at Trapper Creek." We lift it to the ground, then level some planks in the dirt to support it. The tub's made of redwood slats circled by metal bands, only four and a half feet in diameter and four feet high. The tub had made the rounds of Shell during the eighties and ended up at our Beaver Creek house in the last years of our marriage. Joe had the time and patience in the winter to split the tiny pieces of wood it required and to tend the fire through the day to have it ready for evening.

That next night, the girls arrive with their bathing suits and we climb over the edge and sink into the water, stirring the colder water up from the bottom with a tiny wooden paddle. Around us the skies are melting through shades of evening, orange to rose to purple.

"Do you remember the Christmas trees?" I ask and hear them both groan.

"I thought I'd die of embarrassment," Amy says, "scavenging the alleys of Greybull for people's trees. I hardly saw a thing. I had my head down the whole time, afraid one of my friends would see me!"

"Yeah," Jenny adds, "but once we got them home they were pretty cool."

One afternoon after Christmas we'd been in town with the girls in the pickup when Joe saw a discarded tree out by a Dumpster. "You know, that tree's still green and there's no tinsel. It'd look great out by the hot tub." He pulled the pickup

alongside and tossed it in the back, and we began a concerted
scavenge for all we could find. When I came home from work
the next afternoon, the trees had been wired to the fence, the
deck, and each other. Joe had strung white lights around them
all to create a tiny, sparkly forest around the hot tub, with
steam rising up out of it and a fire crackling in its stove.


In the early light I go to the window and look across the hayfields for the foxes, but there's no movement in the space
below the cottonwood or along the ditches in the tall grass
where they hunt mice. Through the morning I come back to
the window again and again, looking, but the landscape's
empty, quiet, and too still without them. I've heard no shots,
and traps wouldn't get them all at once. Poison seems more
likely.

In the late afternoon I'm sweeping the gallery and pass by
the big west window on the opposite side of the schoolhouse
when something catches my eye. *Foxes!* All six of them out in
the tall weeds at the edge of the bluff, not fifty yards away. I
give a whoop and run upstairs for the binoculars. The two
adults sit on their haunches by a mound, and the young ones
romp through the crackling weeds washed clean by last night's
rain. They've moved to safety behind my skirts, and I am
embarrassed by my joy.

That night I leave a little something on the deck, a heel of
French bread, and in the morning it's gone. The next night I
put out some cornbread and by morning it, too, is gone. This
goes against everything I know, but I can't help wanting their
company. I go to town and buy a small bag of expensive lamb

and rice dog food and put a little out each night in a cast-iron skillet, half a cup, not enough to make them dependent. Just a taste, and every morning it's gone.

One evening I'm sitting at my desk with the French doors wide open talking to my mother on the phone as the evening dusk descends and a fox comes to the edge of the deck, watching me. Talking softly, I describe this to my mother. The fox steps up onto the deck and, still watching me, starts eating the dog food. And while I keep talking, my voice low and constant, the fox finishes and steps carefully to the corner and, her back turned, looks out over the creek bottom as the light fades.

In the fall, when Tim's cutting competitions are over for the season, he lets me work his prize-winning Doc O Dynamite cutting mare on a calf in the arena. I've seen him work her plenty of times, riding "turnback" for him as he practiced. He would walk his mare slowly into the bunch of calves at one end of the arena and quietly nudge one out. With his mare positioned squarely before the calf, he'd drop the reins to her neck and let her work to keep it from rejoining the others. As the turnback rider, I'd position myself behind the calf, at a distance, to provide tension and intensity to the workout, to keep the calf from simply drifting back to the other end of the arena.

I step up into the saddle, wanting to stay out of her way, not wanting to be clumsy. Tim talks me through cutting out the calf, moving slowly and quietly with one hand on the saddle horn and the other holding the reins loosely. When Dynamite's facing the calf squarely, her head dropped to his nose level, I drop my rein hand to her neck. He steps to the right, and she smoothly feints left to meet him. Wild eyed, the calf bolts left, and all hell breaks loose underneath me as Dynamite pivots and whirls to stay in front of him, her neck snaked low and ears laid flat to her neck. The saddle falls out from under me as she dives right, then left, and somehow I'm still in the middle, hovering half an inch in the air above her center. The thrill of it has me grinning like a damned fool. When we come to a stop, I howl with delight and plant a kiss on her lathered neck, wishing I could ride life's turns as easily.

For five years my life is divided between two states, with every trip between Utah and Wyoming a paring down of accumulations, books and clothes and furniture and sometimes even friends. Each spring, when the snows are melting in the Wasatch and Salt Lake's in high bloom with flowering crab apples, tulips and daffodils, I pack up and head east and then north toward Kemmerer, where I begin to see bands of sheep scattered across the spare ranges and hear the meadowlarks again. By the time I reach the Big Horn Basin, the calendar has been turned back a month, the buds tightfisted and flurries of snow mixing with sun. Every trip is a shedding, a centering, a test to see how little I can get by with no matter how great the need.

In the early fall of 1998, Jenny's sixteen, almost seventeen, and has been elected junior attendant for the Greybull High School homecoming game. She lets me shop for her while I'm traveling, "something nice," she says, "a dress," and I find her one. A long black dress with cap sleeves and a tie at the back, maybe too elegant for the occasion, but she says she loves it. Amy comes home from college in Laramie and joins me in the bleachers for the game. We buy big bags of popcorn, then wait for halftime and the chance to hoot and holler for our girl.

When the attendants come out onto the field, Jenny's the only one in a dress and she carries it off with great style, escorted by her best friend, Jeremy, an artist, splashy in a bright tie-dyed T-shirt and jeans, his left arm in a cast. As friends they seem fearless, missing the self-consciousness of being boyfriend and girlfriend. In the photograph taken of them after the game, they're all smiles. Her right arm's around his shoulders, and she's pinching his cheek with her left hand as if to say, *Isn't he a doll?*

This fall, with Amy away, Jenny begins showing up at my door at suppertime. I'm surprised at first, as if a wild bird has decided to take up residence on my shoulder, but understand that with her sister gone, she's lonesome. They have always been inseparable, counting on each other first and foremost in a world where their mother could fall off a horse and die, their father could disappear into alcohol, and I could walk away from the home we'd made together. In Amy's presence, Jenny had been the quiet one, adoring and deferring to her. But this fall she spills out words and stories of school and friends, and my jaw drops in amazement at this person I haven't known. I make no sudden moves, lest she fly away.

One weekend we make a quick road trip south to Laramie to see Amy. Another day I take her out of school so we can drive north to Montana to get her braces removed, and she smiles wide and seems to stand taller. We take pictures, and she suddenly has grown into a stunning young woman. Our time together is mostly spent at the Stone School, where she stops often for tea, for dinner, for help with homework. One night she calls to say she's done something to her knee and is wondering what to do. "Do you want me to come over?" I ask. When she doesn't answer, I say, "I'll be right there. Give me a few minutes." Pulling into the driveway, I see the trees we planted have grown sprawling and that the house looks shabby and in need of paint. "Let's ice this knee," I say, "and elevate it. If it's not shipshape by morning, we'll go into the clinic and have them take a look." I get her set up on the couch with ice and pillows, hot tea and a book. "Will your dad be home soon?" I ask. "Yes," she says, "he'll be home soon."

That night I toss and turn with the weight of my choices. The winter's work at Snowbird affords me the luxury of this time and space back in Shell Valley. I depend on it, I tell myself, and she has a father who loves her dearly. I remember Amy's words late one night when I'd been drinking wine and apologized to her for leaving them. She looked me in the eye and said, "But you didn't leave. Look, you're still here." I repeat these words out loud but somehow believe I've chosen wrongly.

It is early November when I close up the schoolhouse and leave the valley. The cottonwoods along Shell Creek have long since gone to gold and shed themselves bare in the wind. The geese have flown south, and the nights have grown cold. I buy Jenny a warm sweater and say, "So come for Christmas this year, you and Amy. Bring your skis." I can see something brighten in her and I drive south with a heavy heart.

. . .

I call Amy and Jenny to remind them of the Christmas invitation. They usually spend Christmas in Minnesota with their grandparents, but I beg and they agree. The promise of skiing at Snowbird helps tip the balance.

In preparation for their visit I retrieve a heavy wooden trunk that's been stored in a friend's basement and discover inside the treasures that have been hidden away all these years: the iris pottery oil lamp, the bird's nest, photographs of my great-grandparents, a few small pieces of artwork, my grandmother's gold bracelet, my arrowhead collection, the Italian slingback heels I can no longer wear. In other boxes I find the hand-blown tulip champagne glasses, the crystal dessert bowls, the Santa pitcher and mugs my mother had given me and the girls. While wind blows and slaps at the loose back gate, I wash the glassware and arrange it around the open kitchen shelves, remembering what it might feel like to have a home again.

In the hours before they arrive, I could wring their necks. They're driving in over the pass in a snowstorm, but they haven't returned phone calls and don't even know for sure how to get to my house, and I can't get off the mountain until mid-evening. After finishing my last massage I check my messages and hear their voices sparkling with excitement. They're hanging out in a university coffee shop waiting for me to get home, not a care in the world.

Jenny has just turned seventeen, on December 11, and Amy twenty, in September. When we hug at the front door, I feel them to be young women, grown out of childhood in the eight weeks since my leaving. They're loaded down with Jenny's skis, Amy's snowboard, coats and duffels with ribbons spilling out through the zippers.

We have a late dinner and tea, then I tuck them into my double bed and curl up in a sleeping bag on the futon next to the Christmas tree in the front room. In the morning I bring them coffee and sit on the bed with them sipping and visiting and soaking them up. These women before me, Amy, bright and shiny, and Jenny, with her shadowy, lidded eyes, now have larger lives in which I'm only a small part.

In the deep fresh powder on the mountain, falling hardly feels like falling at all, so Amy and I are reckless, tumbling happily on one turn after another while Jenny is cautious and slow. Amy gives her a hard time, "Come on, come on, let go and keep up with us. You're too worried about falling."

"Am not."

"Are too!" When she finally catches up to us, she's crusted head to toe in fine white powder, a little snow monster with a grin, and Amy yells, "Let's hear it for Jenny and her very first fall ever!"

When I leave the slopes in the early afternoon to go to work at the lodge, they're free to flirt with all the young boys they tell me about later. Young, cool, hip and so many of them, they say. I leave passes for them at the spa so they can hang out in the hot tub while I finish up my work.

During the days they spend under my wing, we ski and cook and have great meals and laugh. We buy underwear at Victoria's Secret and go to chick flicks, *You've Got Mail* and *Shakespeare in Love.* When Amy and I tear up and laugh at ourselves over a sappy ending, Jenny rolls her eyes and says, "I don't get all this love stuff." Then we tease her mercilessly about her boyfriend, Jason, and make her blush. We do secret shopping and tuck packages under the scraggly Christmas tree; then we sit in the dark with the lights twinkling and drink hot chocolate from the Santa mugs and say this is the most beautiful tree ever.

It's snowing when they leave, and I trot along behind, pushing to help the car up the slight incline of the driveway. Amy's wheels catch the gravel at the road's edge and pull up onto the pavement. They turn and wave, Amy beeping the horn a couple times as they turn away toward their adventure and pick music for the drive home over the pass.

"Be careful!" I yell, waving behind them. "Call me when you get home!"

I stand in the falling snow and watch them pull away up the hill. I've packed them a thermos and sandwiches but know they'll likely stop anyway at the coffee shop by the university because that's a city thing to do and because they're young and delighted with themselves and their beauty. For a few minutes I can imagine clearly where they are and maybe even what they're talking about, as if they're still there under my wing.

As the hours pass I feel them gone. I pick through the photographs we took on Christmas morning with the self-timer, all three of us sitting in front of the tiny tree being silly with bright flowers and Grace staring intently into the sound of the whirring camera. I work through the photographs again and think, *We are still a family, even though we aren't related by blood and don't live in the same house or half the time even in the same state. We are still family, and I will hold on tighter.*

## JENNY

For the first seven miles straight east out of town, she could have closed her eyes and floated off the road into a flat sea of sage. The bitter-smelling stems would have scraped against metal and wakened her to the jolt of hard ground, the pollen rising up around her in a cloud. She could have leaned her head and rested the surprising weight of her seventeen years into the window glass and fallen back to sleep while the car's engine ticked itself cool in the night air. Someone would have come by in the night and taken her home, holding an arm around her shoulder as they knocked at her father's door and raised a call into the darkened house.

Instead, seven miles east of Greybull, the road bore gently to the south and there—I imagine her perfect eyes closed, already dreaming—she and her little brown Toyota stayed the eastern course toward the mountains, crossing the middle line and tumbling end over end down into the only forty-foot embankment in all the fifteen miles of her journey home.

What I discover is this: everyone has their losses.

On that first day of May, my flight from Salt Lake to San Francisco had left at dawn, and I didn't hear the news until I landed in California. In the twenty-four hours before her death, I had emptied my apartment in Salt Lake and loaded everything into the back of my truck and a small U-Haul trailer, then cleaned behind me, erasing all traces of my living there. From those stark rooms, I called Jenny at her dad's and left a message to pass on to Amy, saying I was going to the coast for the weekend and would see them soon. My phone was disconnected at midnight of the last day of April, less than three hours before her accident and four and a half hours before someone driving the highway noticed headlights shining up from the draw.

While our plane descended through the clouds, my friend Paul and I were talking about earthquakes. Circling out over the water, we came back toward the runway so low that the tall marsh grasses beneath us were flattened. Leaning into the window, I thought, *The earth's right there, but we're suspended above it.* I said, "What if we looked down and saw everything shaking, the ground splitting wide open and falling into the ocean. Just think; right now we could pull up and just keep flying."

That day had been spent in Gini and Peter's home, receiving calls from family across the country and piecing together the story of a Friday night party in town and her drive home alone in the early-morning hours. I sat in the stupor of news that didn't make sense and worried for Amy, longing to speak with her. I called her house, her friends, her father, but couldn't find her anywhere. At one point I looked up and three kind faces were looking at me, asking what I needed and did I want to fly back to Salt Lake tonight, head up to Wyoming in the morning? I shook my head and said I couldn't bear the thought of being suspended in air, elbow to elbow with strangers. I wanted to stay the night and hold hands with my friends, then begin the journey in the morning.

When the phone rang, Peter answered and handed it to me, saying softly, "This must be Amy." She must have said the words to ask for me, but I heard nothing after that. I took the phone into the darkened bedroom and spoke to her silence, this precious young woman who'd lost her mother and now her sister. There were no words from her across all the dark miles, and so I spoke as though mine were arms that could gather her up and hold her to me. I heard great gasps of air escaping and moans. I spoke in sounds that had no meaning, only like trees swaying, sounds I would've made to a frightened animal because I didn't know how else to pour out my love.

. . .

For our return trip, Gini and Peter pack for us a small cooler with salami, cheeses, roasted tomatoes, hard bread and a branch of rosemary from their garden, then drop us off at the airport. We hug good-bye, lingering, and walk into the airport, into the buzz and fluorescent lighting and flashing digital displays, and there are hundreds, thousands of people milling around in lines that snake back and forth through the Delta ticket terminal. In the face of this mass I find myself unable to move; I'm a person without skin, an open wound. "I'll wait in line," Paul says. "Why don't you sit down?" I shake my head, the tears coming again now, and move blindly past them all. I find an empty space of counter and lean into it, my head down and one hand over my face and my ticket held out before me in the other. When a man walks by saying, "Ma'am, you'll need to . . ." a hoarse voice says, "My daughter's dead and I need to go home," and he slows, comes back and stands in front of my tears. He gently takes the tickets from my hand and some time later returns them, telling me the gate and the time. "I'm so sorry," he says. "Thank you," I whisper, and we walk away.

Paul drives north with me while I stare out the window. We make it as far as Riverton that night and, after a bruised sleep, begin again in the morning. In Basin, we stop at the funeral home, and I go inside carrying a pair of shoes. I'd been told she was being buried in the black dress I'd bought her for homecoming the fall before. For that occasion she had borrowed these black slides with tall, chunky heels, and I wanted her to wear them again. I wanted to imagine her striding through a spirit world with my shoes on her feet. I wanted to do something for her, to give her one last thing.

In the funeral home I hand them to the director, a kind man and an EMT who'd taught us first aid one winter in the Shell Hall. "Can I see her?" I ask. He shakes his head slightly and pauses. "She's not ready." He disappears through a door and returns a few minutes later with Jenny's black flats, the low heels worn to nubs and the toes scuffed. I take them away with me, holding them in my lap as Paul drives me on to Greybull.

On the marquee in front of Greybull High School, spelled out in square black letters: WE WILL MISS YOU JENNIFER LITTLE. The words seem certain, final, confirmation that this hasn't all been a gross mistake. I had planned to be here in March for Jenny's induction into the National Honor Society, an eight-hour drive up and then back between shifts, but a spring snowstorm blew in, and instead I'd sent a dozen roses. *Congratulations! I'm so proud of you. I'll see you soon.*

We turn down the street toward the trailer where Amy lives with her boyfriend and park among the cars and trucks under the bare trees. We walk past an old wooden table out front, covered with candle wax melted in pools and a scattering of beer cans, and metal folding chairs clustered as though the bodies that filled them had only just gotten up and walked away. Paul squeezes my hand and says, "I'll just hang out here for a while, unless you need me." And I step up onto the rickety porch and knock.

When she opens the door, I see a ghost, a shell. I wrap my arms around her but cannot find her; she's beyond tears, beyond words, all vacant eyes and wisps of hair. She turns away and asks, "Do you want coffee?" The kitchen counter's littered with dishes, casseroles, plates of cookies, a ham, beer cans, coffee cups.

"Yes, I'll get it," but she's already pouring. A handful of her close-knit friends are gathered around the small living room, and they stand and come to me. I feel the flush of my cheek on theirs, the fabric of their shirts under my hands, their clothing covering bodies filled with muscle and heat and blood, still moving, still living. Amy hands me a cup, and we all sit back down as if waiting for something. In the empty space next to her in this uneven circle, I place my hand on her back, looking into her ashen face, and feel her flinch and pull away, and my heart drops into a canyon. Across these miles I have wanted only to be with her, but now that I'm here there's the feeling of conversations already passed among friends, among those who have been at her side. I keep rubbing her back while she stares at the floor because it's all I know to do for her, so far beyond my reach.

There's a knock at the door, and I rise, glad for a job, and let the minister in, a kind-looking man in flannel and boots whose son is already here. He leans to give Amy a hug and whispers in her ear, and I see tears gather behind the strands of hair in her face. He talks about the service the following day, giving us a sense of how the day will go. We nod, following his directions, and when he leaves, I move to the door and motion Paul inside. We wash dishes, sweep the floors, fill trash bags, wipe counters, heat and set out food, trying to be helpful.

. . .

The viewing is held in the late afternoon on a side street in Greybull in a small white house surrounded by homes with sidewalks and big cottonwood trees just leafing out. Joe's older brother from San Antonio stands quietly against the wall in the front room, a presence there with her body. Joe's mother comes up and squeezes my hand and speaks to me in a hushed voice, her deep Texas accent. "We found a corduroy jacket for her little arms—they couldn't fix them—and I think it's okay with the dress." This last part tentative, almost a question, and I look into her pleading face and say, "Yes, I'm sure it is. I'm so glad you were here to do this for her."

I remain at the entrance to the small room that holds her coffin, the walls and carpet all cream and light, waiting to feel my feet settle on the ground and my heart catch up to this place, this day, this moment. But it never comes, that feeling, and so I move up to see her laid out there as though only briefly gone, perhaps asleep, an ill moment she hopes to nap away before a special evening. I want to reach out and run my fingers along the smooth olive of her skin, but I do not, cannot. I study her closed eyes, her eyebrows delicate and feathered above, the blush of her cheeks, the pale-rose gloss on her lips. But in her presence my tears have disappeared. I'm a dried-up spring, a river gone underground. I stifle an urge to turn back to the room and laugh, *Isn't this the craziest thing you have ever seen?* but then find myself looking for her feet, the shoes. Her lower half is covered in white satin and she's in her black dress, the one I'd taken from the rack at Whippy Bird in Lander and tried on to see if it fit because we're so much the same size and then brought to her and tied the back sash and said "Oh my god, you are one lovely girl," and she'd turned and swirled the skirt around her, so pleased with what she could see in the tall mirror propped against my bedroom wall. I reach out and touch the corduroy of her jacket, black with brass snaps and some good measure of West in it, and I think, *Well, yes, this was a good choice to cover her little arms,* and wonder what it is beneath the sleeves, what it is that couldn't be fixed from her flying through the window, her seat belt dangling limp behind her.

On the sidewalk beneath old trees I see her boyfriend, Jason, and put my arms around him while his body shakes. "I gave her roses that night and told her I loved her," he says. "I bet she hated that," I say, and that makes him laugh. "Yeah, she did hate the mushy stuff." I step back and hold his hands and say, "I am so glad she had you. I'm so glad that she had you to hold her and be good to her before she died."

I remember that day late in the fall after homecoming when we'd gone together to see a doctor at the clinic between Greybull and Basin. I'd asked, awkwardly, if she'd had sex yet, and she answered, slowly, "No, but we've talked about it." I said, "I'm afraid for you, afraid in the way I am for all of us. Sex leaves you so vulnerable, and if it doesn't, that's even worse. But I want you to be ready, and I won't be here to help." She'd nodded and said that's what she wanted, so we went together to have her examined and get a prescription for birth control. "When you're ready, you'll know and you'll make a good decision, and this is what I can do to help from far away." The woman doctor had looked at me hard, as though demanding to know what I was thinking, and then spoke to me alone and almost made me cry, but I said, "This is what I can do. This is what we're doing." In the following months, I'd asked Jenny about it, but even over the miles, even on the phone in the living room whose long cord wound up the staircase, she was too shy to say.

It is dusk when Paul and I leave, driving east on the highway toward the ranch where Stan and Mary have offered beds to my family. At the curve, we slow and stop and walk to the reflector post above the wash on the far side of the road. Ribbons, yellow and white, are tied to it in bows, the tails hanging down loose, and flowers in bunches, daisies, roses and lilacs, here and there sage and some evergreen. Piled around the base are round river stones and flat moss rock from the hills. More flowers, bare-stemmed or wrapped in green florist tissue or clear cellophane from the grocery, are laid at the base, tucked in among the stones to hold them from the wind. In a Budweiser can there's a cluster of Indian paintbrush, crimson, yellow and rose, brought in from the hills.

We climb the narrow stairs to the garret bedrooms, choose one, and Paul holds me through the night, not talking, not asking anything of me. The curtains at the open window by our heads move through all the hours, sucking to the screen with the night winds and then billowing a raw chill back across us.

"Do you want it closed?" he asks.

"No." The curtains ripple to momentary stillness, a sigh, a

whisper. The stars shine. From downstairs, the sound of someone up in the night. "Paul?"

"Yes."

"What if I hadn't left?"

"Shhhh." His soft breath's warm at my ear. He pulls the thin covers up over us. "People die even when you stay." It's silent for a while. "Can you sleep?"

"No." My tongue on the roof of my mouth, a puff of air releases it and forms the sound.

"Do you want to talk?"

"No." A sigh, a whisper. "Just this for now."


At dawn I wrap myself in a wool blanket and sit on the floor by the bed, writing. Paul slips downstairs for coffee, and I hear the sounds of my parents' voices, distant, soft, and others as he joins them. With words on paper come tears, and when he sets a mug of coffee on the floor beside me, I'm blinded with them.

"They ask how you are, if you're coming down."

I shake my head silently, unable to imagine how this day can proceed, too sad for social graces.

"I'll let them know."

"Paul, this day's going to be weird for you, all these people you don't know. But will you just stay close to me?"

"Yes," he says.

"Even with family and everything, you'll stay within reach?"

"Yes."

. . .

The cottonwoods along the ditch below the road have grown immense, sprawling, from the bundled seedlings I'd planted in the early years of our marriage. The stacked poles of the round corral have lost their bark and gone smooth, silvered now in the morning light. "Here," I say, "this is the turn," and I see a man with a shovel draining irrigation water away from where it's pooled across the drive. He looks old and bent and heavy, and I try to place him, this person who'd be at the house on this day. When we pass beneath the gateposts and cross the uneven cattle guard, he turns and raises a hand in greeting, holding it midair as we approach. I see under the ball cap that it's Joe and wonder how I could have missed this before. Moving slowly past, I reach through the open window, and he squeezes my hand. "I'm so glad you're here," he says and follows the pickup down the drive to this place I used to call home.

My brother and his family pull in behind us with our parents, who flew in the day before from a conference in Maine. Along Beaver Creek the willows are leafing out and full of birdsong and gurgling water, the sounds of early spring incongruous with the day that faces us. Joe leans his shovel against the tack shed and offers his hand to each of us, closing his arms around me, and in his lingering I can feel the man I used to know, the man I fell in love with, alive beneath his skin. I cannot imagine his loss, yet old resentments fly up around me, requiring little to set them loose. *Were you drinking? Did you know where she was or when she'd be home?* I do not say these words in this pause of embrace and never will. The one who walked away, I don't have the right.

We walk the gravel drive together, under the overhang with the moose paddles that Amy had found riding on the mountain with him the summer of the Yellowstone fires. I can see Jenny there under the piñata hung for Amy's birthday, her eyes blindfolded with a scarf, twirling and whacking and laughing with her head tilted back, and all around a dirty yellow smoke drifting across the basin from the wildfires. Along the fence below the gate, the wild plum thicket has grown tangled and is creeping out into the yard just as the catalogue had warned it would when I pored over it one winter, imagining abundance and not believing that anything could grow too much in such a spare place.

When we step up onto the stone terrace, I walk through memories of Jenny and Amy carving pumpkins, stringing Christmas lights up into the trees, laying out on beach towels and working on their tans in the earliest summer sun. We go through the door into the living room that smells faintly of stale grease, Comet, and woodsmoke. With our sorrows sharp and our words unsaid, we gather around the minister and gratefully close our eyes against this day as he leads us in a prayer. When I raise my head, I see that we're all still here, gathered for the worst possible reason, like shards of glass piled together.


The Shell Hall is a cavernous log structure where the community shares Easter breakfasts and Halloween chili suppers, dances at weddings and grieves for its dead. With our lights on we trail one another down the hill into town; cars and trucks line both sides of the streets in every direction, and two yellow school buses sit empty, their doors open. We park in the spaces left for us and stand together, hesitant, a disparate group safe in this fragile moment together when inside there are so many. I reach out for Paul's arm and let him lead me in behind Amy and Joe. I see my mother's face turn as if she's looking for her place, but I can't help, and Carol falls in at her side and takes her in with Dad and my brother following. I'm aware of the floor as we walk, the polish of old wood laid in thin strips and of the rows and rows and rows of people sitting in folding chairs. I can't see their faces, don't even look, but can feel the heat of all their bodies.

When we're seated, the stage in front of us is filled with Jenny's classmates, seated or standing all around the edges, and in every space there are flowers and ribbons in colors brighter than anything growing in this country, raised up in tall vases and on pedestals around and behind the closed coffin as though to bear us up, to keep us from sinking to the ground.

While the minister speaks, I study the weave of Joe's jacket in front of me, Amy leaning into his shoulder. I reach out and touch the fabric at his shoulder, this man who was once my husband, and offer up a silent apology for all I have not been to him. Jenny's friends stand and speak, Fred with his cow-licked hair and then Kaycee in her grandmother's bright red coat, their words floating over us across the room: *laughter, kindness, goofy, sparkling, karate chop, glow in the dark.* I watch their faces and envy them their days of jostling through crowded hallways with her and sharing bus seats, their memories of her last day.

Joe's brother stands up and sings, all alone with just his voice.

*Remember me when the candle lights are gleaming.*
*Remember me at the close of a long, long day.*
*And it would be so sweet when all alone I'm dreaming*
*Just to know you still remember me.*

He sings to us out in the open, away from the podium and the microphone, standing with his hands clasped loosely in front of him and his head tilted back, his eyes closed, singing for Jenny, for Amy, for this brother he loves so much.

When it's my turn to stand and face the room, I see there are people standing in the aisles, spilling out the doorways, and leaning through the open windows. I see the faces of friends, of parents and teachers who'd shepherded one another's children to safety, the tears now welling in their eyes, holding each other, and I wonder how one can speak the words out loud without howling at the loss.

In the seats right in front of me, Amy sits with her head sunk to her knees and her father with his head bowed in grief. Next to them are Amy and Jenny's grandparents and aunts from Minnesota, her grandmother from Texas, my mother and father, my brother and his wife. Midway down on the far side, Jenny's friend Kaycee is sitting in her bright red coat, her face beaming at me as if to say, *Yes, you can do this, Laura. Come on, I'll help you.*

"What I've discovered these last days is that the conversation of death is filled with the language of love.

"All of you here, know that you are precious. Know that you count.

"Amy, know that you are a sweet and golden light in this world and that we offer up our hearts to help you heal.

"Jenny, take our love and grow wings.

"We pray that you have found the arms of your mother.

"We wish that we could have loved you longer and more.

"Today we have to trust that our love was enough."


The Whaley Cemetery sits west of Beaver Creek Road at the edge of the Diamond Tail hayfields, where in early May only a few cattle are grazing with their late calves. This day the tall iron gates are swung open, and we move through them on foot, through grass coming up with spring and through markers of lives past, the chill winds gusting around us. We follow where we're led, to a place near the back by the barbed wire fence, old cottonwoods rising out of the irrigation ditch that runs alongside. We move as one to the freshly dug ground with a mound of earth behind and, at head and foot, two young crabapple trees blooming weakly, thin and yielding to the winds. Flowers are piled up, their tender petals not meant to last the raw. My mother stands off to one side, arms crossed, shivering in her thin jacket and my father's hands on her shoulders. A face appears from the many, the husband of a friend, and takes off his winter coat and wraps it around my mother. I'm grateful for that as I have nothing to give her, no extra solace or warmth of any kind. Across the way, in a place I can't reach her, Amy's long hair is blowing, her face down and her hand in her father's and her uncle close behind them, standing watch over them. A service is spoken, but I don't hear the words, can't remember them, only the cold and how the bodies blocked the wind as they came closer and gathered around us.

## MOVING CAMP

---

In the dark of morning the lights of Far Valley Ranch shine in
haloes over the corrals and barn. The air is damp and sweet
with the smell of new grass and red-clay hills. As I park my
pickup, Press appears in the circle of barnyard light, leading
haltered horses to the pole fence, where he ties them alongside
the rest of the string. I find a currycomb and brush and start on
one end and in the dim light work through the horses, some
familiar to me from years past, others new. Eighteen of these
twenty have been leased from a Pavillion rancher who runs
over a thousand head on the bare ranges of the Wind River

Indian Reservation during the winter, when they paw through snow for dried grass and winterfat. In the spring he works them through corrals and sorts them to outfitters and guest ranches across the state and beyond, delivered in a clatter from the backs of semitrailers.

Once the horses leave the ranch this morning, heading into the mountains, they won't return until next year. Guests will come and go from town, as we will, but the horses will trail as a group from camp to camp, leapfrogging from trailhead to trailhead from the East Fork of the Wind River west and north into Yellowstone Park and the early snows of fall

Press whistles through the saddling, his long legs covering ground back and forth between horses. "That sorrel with the high withers is gonna need the number seven saddle and an extra pad. And let's put a pack saddle on the new bay mare this trip to see how her manners are. Biscuit, my man, looks like you made it another year. Looking fine, looking fine."

When the horses are brushed and saddled, I fall back to the work shed where wooden panniers are already packed with canned goods and spices from the day before. I open the refrigerators and load insulated panniers with apples and oranges, cabbage, iceberg lettuce, cucumbers, carrots, onions, and celery, then fill the hard-sided coolers with frozen brownies, cookies, ground beef, ham, bacon, sausage, steaks, and chicken, tucking Miracle Whip, mustard, and a small bottle of penicillin for the horses into one of them. With hand scales I lift each packed pannier by the leather loops and balance it with the weight of its mate, adding and removing items, and when they match, I carry them out and set them as a pair in the dawning light. My blood is pumping, my step quick and sure. I find myself relieved to be moving and doing what I know how to do, without thinking, to leave the paralyzing territory of grief behind me.

After the funeral, I'd driven to the small town of Dubois in the valley between the southern Absarokas and the Wind River Range and unloaded my belongings into a few rooms at the back of a friend's garage. Two large windows of this makeshift apartment opened directly into the corral of an ancient white horse and beyond, due south, to slopes where snows still flurried and spring seemed a long time away. When the last box was inside, I found a patch of light on the couch and lay down. Every day the old horse would hang his head against the other side of the window glass, inches from mine on the pillow, his lip quivering as he dozed, dreaming of oats or tender grass or maybe the branch of rosemary warming to fragrance on my side, beyond his reach. He stood for hours against the dark stained logs of our shared wall, soaking up the sun and sheltering from the wind. Through another window behind the couch, black-capped chickadees fussed among pale-budded hedges and scattered the sunflower seeds I'd left out for them. Between these two windows, south and west, the sun threw light on me most of the day.

When Amy came, I set up my table in the living room and gave her massage in the sun with the horse at the window and Grace napping at my feet. Beneath my hands she was pale and quiet. There was the sound of our breath, of birds chattering at the feeder, of a lawn mower somewhere in the distance, as I moved over her slowly, gently, knowing that whatever pain

I felt was only a sliver of hers. When she turned over onto her back, tears slipped from her eyes and she wiped them away.

When I finished, I put the tea kettle on the stove while she wrapped a robe around herself and settled, dazed, on the couch. I brought the tea and sat beside her. I asked her how she was doing, and she could not say. As the afternoon light blazed and faded, I asked about the night of Jenny's death, the party, and she shook her head in silence. Maybe it was only to me she couldn't say the words, but I didn't press. It was enough to have her close, to make her tea and keep her warm. One would think there'd be so many words to say and maybe for some there are but not for us. Without Jenny we are strangers. Without Jenny we are everything to each other, what we have left.

When finally packed and moving, we line out single file, a string of eight riders and twenty horses with all that we need for the week: duffels, sleeping bags, books, medicine, extra horseshoes, food and kitchen all loaded into metal or canvas panniers and hanging from the cross bucks of each horse's pack saddle. Each load's covered with a generous square of green canvas mantie tucked so neatly under the edges with exacting diamond hitches that the horses heading up the trail look to be carrying Christmas presents.

In our early trips, the high passes will be corniced in snow. Later, the flies will bite, and by early August, there will be thunderstorms in the afternoon. When we reach the Yellowstone River Valley in the early fall, a thin glaze of ice will cap the water bucket in the morning. Bull elk will raise antlered heads within dark timber and bugle in the dusky hours and through the night. At dawn we'll hear the deep, gravelly cries of sandhill cranes long before they appear, flying the river bottom on long silvered wings.

It feels like a betrayal, heading into the mountains with these strangers, and I'm afraid I can't do what it takes to walk among the living and leave her behind.

My place this season is bringing up the end of the pack string, riding a long-legged bay gelding named Waffle and leading Maggie, Irene, Biscuit and Trooper. I pick up dropped gloves and hats speared by low-hanging branches. I tighten loose cinches and point out king's crown, scarlet penstemon, lacy wild carrot and the tracks of grizzly bears. But mostly, in the rear of the string, it's quiet and private, and I'm left to my own thoughts.

At the Campbell Creek camp we wake to fog. I'd dreamt that a hand was laid on my shoulder, a voice saying that everything would be okay. I try to remember more when I wake, but it's gone and only the feeling of being touched by peace remains. By the time the horses are packed and tied into strings, the fog has burned off and we ride out into the sunlight.

When I look back at the camp we're leaving, I see only the shadows of where we've been and what we've done. The sod we dug up in heavy clumps for the fire pit has been pieced back together in the hole and covered with two buckets of water dipped from the stream, so once again alpine fescue and wild yarrow bloom there. The firewood has been stashed under low, drooping branches of evergreens. Horse droppings have been kicked and scattered to decompose. On the hard ground where we slept curled under canvas, there's only the faintest impression of occupancy, with stems of grass already rising back.

Marsh marigold, prairie smoke, miner's lettuce, wild strawberries. At the campfire I dish up hash browns and grilled pork chops with mustard and thyme. I pour fresh coffee for guests balanced on logs with plates in their laps. I nod, listening to stories of the jobs they're retiring from, the empires they've created. I become the daughter they haven't spoken to, the wife who no longer seems much interested. I listen and nod and, invisible, become the mirror they look into to judge their lives.

I have lost someone I love and am full of regret. Pouring coffee seems a small penance to win my way back to solid ground.

It's almost dusk as the pack string falls downslope into the Dead Horse Meadows camp, the horses stumbling their loads side to side. From the guests, a hopeful murmur rises when they realize their first long ride's almost over. Press circles the lead horses and calls out, "Dinner, one hour!" and, whistling, begins to loosen ropes and unload packhorses.

Our guests, two couples from Georgia, dismount on rubbery legs, pull their tents and duffels from the piles and pack them off into the meadow to locate the perfect spot to pitch them. I begin setting the kitchen up for dinner and out of the corner of my eye see David out in the meadow on hands and knees, feeling the ground for lumps. Flossie stands above him with arms spread wide, pivoting around to locate the best view.

Tents are placed to catch the morning sun on the sheer rock face or to capture the sound of running water. Each will house the dreams of its inhabitants, what's missing from their lives, what they hope for, and inside is the peace that descends each night when they lay themselves down, sore and worn from a world that blisters their hands, pulls their muscles, roughs their skin and reminds them they're living among bears that could eat them. For some reason, this gives comfort to us all.

Later, under cover of the kitchen fly, I fall asleep in the firelight and wake in the night to hear the deep howling of wolves on the far ridges, somber, mournful, nothing like the brash young sounds of coyotes. I lift my head, listening until there's nothing but silence.


Three trips into our summer, and two days from our trailhead at the Double Cabins on the East Fork, we take a day ride up through stringer meadows toward Mount Kent. Christi, our wrangler on this trip, rides with us. And Boo and Bill, a jolly couple from Minnesota I've come to enjoy. Last night we sang a little and jitterbugged around the fire.

Also with us is Camille, a small, lovely Georgian in her seventies who'd grown up riding hunter jumpers. She comes out of her tent every morning looking completely unruffled, as though she'd slept on the ground every night of her life. On our first day out of the trailhead, she'd fallen to the back of the string and had ridden alongside me through the open meadows. When she asked about my life, I told her that my stepdaughter had been killed in a car accident only eight weeks before. "Oh," she said, "I'm so sorry. It must be a comfort, though, to have so much life around you," and she raised a gloved hand to the trees.

For nearly two hours out of camp we follow faint game trails, gaining elevation, until we reach a lower summit ridge of Mount Kent. From here, the climb becomes steep and rocky. We stop, and the others walk on in hopes of seeing elk in the snowfields on the other side. Camille and I stay behind with the horses.

We sit on the rocks with our lunches and binoculars, tiny yellow stonecrop and alpine phlox at our feet, the world spread out before us. At this altitude the air's so thin it seems to quiver. We can see the high ridges along the boundary of the reservation, Castle Mountain, Steamboat Mountain and, to the south, the Wind River Range covered in snow.

From beneath her draped sun hat, Camille looks at me and says, "You never get over it." I lean forward to hear her and see that there are tears in her eyes, see this even though the wind is blowing and the sun is strong and the human face seems not part of the view.

"I lost my first-born child when he was nine months old," she says. "That was forty years ago. Time changes things, but you never get over it."

In early August, we camp for two nights at Swain's Riffle on the Upper Yellowstone River. The morning is wet, the willows dripping with the mists of low hanging clouds. There are only three guests this trip, Bob and Judy, a couple from Oklahoma, and Anna, their newly arrived exchange student from Germany. A year older than Jenny, she's wide-eyed and game, never once complaining about the long hours in the saddle. She has Jenny's olive skin and her sweet, even temperament. I find myself watching her, lingering over her movements.

Grizzly tracks crisscross this valley. We camp among trees with bark shredded by their claws and picnic at the edge of willow bottoms where piles of scat stand like monuments, markers that speak more of ownership than any line on a map. A closer look reveals pieces of moths, chokecherry pits, clumps of hair, and sometimes shards of bone, depending on place, season, and what's available for them to eat.

In the soft earth, we spot grizzly tracks, the first Anna has seen, and Press gets down from his horse to show her, tracing a finger in the air above them and explaining how they differ from those of a black bear. What they have in common are the parts: pad, toes, claws. But the grizzly pad has a flatter outline across the top, its little toe nearly even with the next, while the black bear's is more rounded, with its little toe dropped below. Unmistakable are the marks left by the claw tips, sprung around the toes like a half halo in the earth. A grizzly's claws are half again the length of a black bear's. The hind prints of both look unsettlingly like a human foot.

Our trail down to the lower Yellowstone is jackstrawed

with dead timber, burned in the Mink Creek fire of 1988. We snake the horses around the splintered ends of downed trees and lunge them over top of the low ones. In between and under these silvered trunks are acres of magenta fireweed dotted with tender green aspen seedlings and clumps of feathery alpine fescue. What had once been a dark, thick monoculture of lodgepole pine is now a sunlit tangle of decaying timbers and new growth.

We are following Yellowstone's South Boundary Trail up Lynx Creek toward Mariposa Lake when we emerge from the trees to see a grizzly sow feeding along the creek with her two cubs. She rises up from them, blindly alarmed, and paws the air that carries our scent. She woofs at her cubs, and they draw up close under her shadow. Risen up, she stands ready to protect them. Risen up, she is tender and fierce like love that can tear out your heart or heal it.

In early September, the three-lobed leaves of skunkbush along Shell Creek are turning to cranberry and the willows to gold. With a couple of days' break from the mountains, I drive up to Shell to meet Amy at her dad's house. She sits across the floor from me, a young woman of twenty, surrounded by piles of clothes. Her blond hair has grown stringy and needs to be cut, but she has some color back in her cheeks and a softness in her voice. We're in the long attic bedroom with its sloping eaves that she used to share with Jenny. We pull clothes from the drawers and closet and sort them piece by piece into piles for each of us, for her close friends, the thrift store and the Shell dump. We both admit that we'd been dreading this task but find it oddly soothing to be doing something physical about her loss.

We begin as though we're digging a grave, and each choice is hard. We linger over junior-high sweaters and motley T-shirts. When Amy holds up a lime-green polyester shirt with huge lapels, we finally crack up. "Oh my god, this is just awful. What was she thinking?" This one's tossed into the thrift store pile, followed by another and another. We weep for our loss and laugh because we don't know what else to do, and the piles grow more quickly.

When we finish in the late afternoon, my pickup's filled with black garbage sacks of clothes for the thrift store, a half-dozen years' worth of cross-country skis with their little boots, red and yellow and blue. We saved treasures for ourselves, for her dad, for her friends, and we're tired but lightened.

I wonder what it is that we clear a space for. Of what possible use is this empty space created by loss?

It's mid-September, our last trip of the season, and we're camped in a thin scattering of trees at the edge of Basin Creek Meadows, a few miles below Heart Lake. The grasses along the creek are tall and turning to browns and yellows, bending deeply over the pools at each meander of the stream. At night we hear the howls of wolves. Early mornings we're wrapped in an icy blanket of fog, sunk in silence that hangs low across the basin. When the sun burns through and the skies clear, great shining loops of spiderwebs are left hanging from the tree branches and hot pools across the basin send up drifts of steam.

We have packed in ten women from a Jackson Hole conservation group, and the conversation leans toward the racy and lighthearted. They're vibrant women, artists and hikers, and I find myself drawn to them. Warned of the chance of early snow, they've come prepared with layers of fleece, pack boots and flasks for their ritual before-dinner happy hour. Among us all there is an air of celebration.

One evening just as we're finishing dinner and circled close around the fire, a young boar grizzly appears in the meadow at the edge of camp, pawing in the tall grasses and digging up small roots. Speaking in whispers, we tiptoe for cans of pepper spray and binoculars and watch him in the last silvery light. He doesn't look up. We watch as though there's some invisible barrier between us, but any one of us imagines a scene in which he lifts his head and walks toward camp.

As the minutes pass, we grow louder, bolder, and still he doesn't look up. Then it's time to unsaddle horses and turn them free for the night, which we do, attaching bells around the necks of half of them. They go to their knees and roll on their backs in the tall grass, and even then the bear does not look up. The horses wander off, a clanging chorus in the dusk, and finally, when it's almost too dark to see, the bear simply turns and ambles away, crossing the creek at a wide, shallow crossing, and heads east across the meadow.

I finish the dishes by headlamp and pull the food panniers up their ropes onto the bear pole. My tent's set off by itself near where we last saw the bear, but when I crawl into my sleeping bag, I'm too tired to care.

From my duffel, I pull out pages that Jenny had written only weeks before her accident. The topic the students in her English class had been given was their own imagined deaths, and they were asked to describe how they'd be missed by loved ones and what their hopes had been for their lives. I imagine that the assignment was meant to highlight the importance of each young life, but the irony is hard to take.

Her nine pages are handwritten, with lines crossed out and words inserted with arrows. This clear window into her heart is unsettling, not least because the death she imagined comes in a car accident. She's driving down Shell Canyon and headed home in the night when a rockslide sends her careening off a cliff. *That weightless feeling you get on a roller coaster only 1,000 times more intense comes over my entire body and fear seemed to engulf me. It made me want to scream and laugh at the same time. Janis was still singing "Me and Bobby McGee" on the radio as I fall to my death. I could hear my dad downstairs making a drink. I wanted to go tell him that I was home but I knew I wouldn't be here long. I couldn't stand to think of what will happen to him. He will just give up. He will no longer be able to get close to people for fear of losing them. I see him taking his horse and riding away and never being seen again.*

She says she'll miss her sister the most and that it would be hardest for Amy because she can't run away from it and will have to face her death every day of her life. Jenny then writes about her friend Jeremy and how she'll miss their early-morning phone conversations about how to take over the world.

Of her desire to finish college, she writes, *I planned on becoming a world traveler so I could be more certain of my decisions. I wanted to be a photographer so I could remember every*

*moment of it and share my experience and wisdom.* She writes,
*I see a picture of my relatives and me and realize I have a great
relationship with lots of people.*

She offers a small piece of advice: *Don't take anything for
granted. Everything in your life is there for a reason and if you
ignore it, you will miss out on a lot.*

My name isn't anywhere in the piece, not as someone she
felt responsible for or depended on. Months after the accident,
when I read these pages to a friend, she said, "But Laura, I hear
you in every word."

By the twentieth of September, the nights are long, and there
isn't enough light to find the horses until nearly seven in the
morning. I shut off my alarm and pull my jeans and fleece
from the bottom of my sleeping bag where they've stayed
warm through the night. There's a hard frost on the ground
and the smell of snow in the air. I can see a flashlight moving
through the dark toward the highline where the two wrangle
horses are tied.

By seven thirty, the coffee has come to a boil, the Dutch
oven full of bacon is beginning to sizzle, and the horses have
been brought in, bells clanging, for morning grain. By eight,
Press and his help have caught and saddled most of the horses,
and I'm yelling, "Breakfast! Breakfast!" to ladies pulling on
their boots or still deep in their sleeping bags. It's move day,
our last of the season, and it feels as if we'll be leaving on the
front side of a storm.

By nine, the kitchen fly gets dropped to the ground and
duffel bags are piled up at the edge of camp, where we'll pack

the horses. Tents are dropped and rolled, still frosty and stiff, into canvas bags. "Last call for coffee!" And what's left is poured into the fire pit. "Last call for the latrine!" And I head to the woods with a shovel to fill in the hole and bring back the roll of toilet paper. We scatter firewood, kick horse piles apart and comb the ground for bits of foil or debris.

Within hours, the camp that had been raised and cultivated into our home is simply gone, measured into even loads on either side of the packhorses. Next to each load, I throw a lash cinch and a canvas mantie and, for the hard-sided ones, an extra Decker pad. The ladies are done packing their duffels now and are holding horses, jerking the off-side lash ropes tight while Press whistles through the work. Diamonds are tied, the pack strings get half-hitched together, and then we're moving out from our last camp as snowflakes begin to fall from the sky.

The campfire we're leaving will be cold for the winter, blanketed under snow and visited by bears, wolves, raccoons and elk passing through, headed to lower winter ranges. I imagine the life that closes in neatly behind us, the tracks crossing the open meadows telling a story that's not ours to hear. It seems to me a sort of spirit world, outside of my knowing, and I want to imagine Jenny here, too, passing in long, joyful strides on her way through, moving in silence with her wise eyes like the bear or cackling and laughing like the women lined out in front of me.

We jump the horses over a boggy creek crossing on the northwest edge of the meadow, and I turn in my saddle to check the packs of my string. Cross bucks upright, ropes tight, nothing dangling. I look back at the trees where we camped and see that the snow's already sifting the greens and browns and yellows into its own winter shades. Across the meadow to the east, where just the day before we'd sunbathed on warm rock slabs by the hot springs, white steam rises in the cold air and the silvered trunks of burned trees catch the snow.

## HEART MOUNTAIN

Coming out of the mountains in the fall after Jenny's death, grief lands back in my lap. When the reason to move every day is gone, I can't find another. When I think the ash of every sorrow has burned cold, I'm mistaken. So when my sister comes and bundles me north to Cody, I let her take me, and when my family proposes a hike to the top of Heart Mountain, I lace up my boots.

From the bottom gates, we hike several hours on the faint two-track road with a steady and heart-pounding grade toward the mountain's steepest slopes. It is mid-October, and panicles of Indian ricegrass are sprung open like fireworks. Tall clumps of Great Basin wildrye rustle in the breeze. We climb through sagebrush benches and limber pine to find ourselves in groves of silver-barked aspen, their golden leaves driven to ground in patches of early snow. In the last hour's steep pitches, we move nearly hand over fist through snow and rock and small trees that slant from the wind.

When we climb out of the trees, the summit is bare and open with gravel and limestone in a shock of bright sunlight. I stand with my arms stretched wide, drying the sweat from my body, and spin a slow circle like a radar disk scanning the terrain from this dizzying height. The Absarokas and the Beartooths and, toward the east, the Pryors and the Big Horns. To the south, the rose-hued McCullough Peaks in the foreground and the distant haze of the Owl Creek range. From here, it seems the tracks of my entire adult life are visible, scratched out across this landscape that has been my constant, more sure than any man's touch, less frail than the walls of any home.

We drop to the limestone slabs and pull food and water from our packs, peel oranges and divide ham sandwiches among us. We stretch our aging, achy bodies. An eagle rises from beneath the cliff. After a summer spent with strangers, the familiar presence of my family is a balm.

From an empty space amid the conversation around me, I am uncovered to tears. "I'm stalled out and don't know what step to take next," I hear myself say. "I'm tired of moving, of carrying everything with me. I want a home, but I don't know where it is." For a moment it's silent, and then I say, "I don't know what to do."

The wind picks up and billows the jackets strewn around

us. I pull my hands away from my face and see that my brother and sister and niece are still there with me, quiet, listening. My sister lays a hand on my shoulder and rubs my back. "It's all right," she says. "You'll know."

That night I dream that something large and awful is after me. I run into a big glass gazebo with round glass walls and leafy trees both inside and out. I pull the door shut behind me and run through another circle of glass walls, out of breath, and close that door behind me, too, pressing my face to the glass. Through the leaves I see a dark shadow on the outside of the farthest glass. I hear its breath and know it can see me, know that the walls are thin and I am small. I realize that if I open up my lungs like a bellows, I'll become loud, and that the louder I am, the larger I'll grow. With my voice, I can become big and save myself.

My sister, sleeping next to me, shakes me awake, frightened by the sounds I'm making in the night. "Like the wind," she says. "Like a wild thing howling."

I don't know for sure, but I think I would have beaten it.


There among the rocks that day, so close to the sky, my words must have stirred the wind. It wasn't long before there was news of a position opening up with a conservation organization that had just bought Heart Mountain Ranch and planned to open an office in Cody. Against my crazy-quilt résumé, the job description looked daunting, but they offered me the position, telling me they needed someone who knew the country and understood the ranches.

So within months I have a home in the shadow of Heart Mountain and my days are filled with migration corridors, winter ranges, rivers, landowners and a life back in the land that has carved me.

One day, I make arrangements to ride with the manager of the Two Dot Ranch, a sprawling, fifty-thousand-acre cattle ranch on the northern Absaroka slopes and a critical haven for wildlife. "I want to show you our sagebrush projects back up country," Mark says, "but we've had something come up, and I need to help these guys get our bulls moved before I can go. Do you mind coming with us? Or would you rather wait for another day?"

"Not at all. I'm here to visit and see the country, and as long as we're horseback I'm happy." I unload my saddle from the pickup and lift it onto the tall bay mare he points out for me. "That's my wife's horse. She'll do dressage or cut cattle or anything. And she'll take good care of you."

We trailer the horses north to where seventeen bulls are scattered along Neumeyer Creek. We split up to go to work, and trotting out, I can feel a smile spreading across my face, and the sense of being at home and in place.

Once we've gathered the bulls to the road and are trailing along behind, Mark says, "These guys have something they want to ask you." The two ranch hands are smiling like Cheshire cats.

"So, you like wolves?" the younger one asks, cocky and certain that he doesn't.

Mark glances at me in apology but is swallowing a grin himself.

"Sure I like wolves." That snaps their heads around, ready for an argument.

"Well!"

"But I like cows, too. Without cows, you don't have ranches. And without ranches, you don't have winter ranges. I'm more of a middle-of-the-road kind of person."

"So, you aren't a tree hugger?"

"I actually like trees quite a lot."

When a bull feints back on us going through the gate, my horse dives and gets around him. The hands look at me as if I might not be completely worthless after all, and I feel a flush of happiness for this day—for the horse under my saddle, for cowboys who love to argue about wolves, for the country spread out around me once again as far as I can see.

Amy calls to say that she's coming over to Cody and has something she wants to talk about. In the year since Jenny's death, she and her boyfriend have moved into her father's house, and she's been working at a Western-wear store in Greybull, sometimes waitressing, treading water in her grief. Having never particularly liked this young man, I've worried about her and made myself available, but this is the first time she has asked.

She sits across from me at the restaurant wearing a paisley scarf I'd given her and dangling silver earrings. Her hair's long and unkempt, but I see a bit of brightness in her face and can tell a question's waiting to be asked even as she studies the menu. When our wine arrives and we've ordered, I say, "So what's up?"

"Well." She hesitates. "Ryan's taking a construction job in Indiana and asked me to go with him." Her cheeks flush with color and her eyes open up with the first sign of hope I've seen. "What do you think?"

"What would you do?"

"Waitress, probably, something easy for a while. What do you think about Dad?"

"Oh, Amy, your dad loves you. The last thing in the world he wants is for you to stay and take care of him. Ask him. I'm sure he'd say the same thing." I watch her eyes glisten as she fiddles with her ring.

"So, what about me? Do you think this is a good thing or a mistake?"

"Well, it's a dead-end job in Indiana. And he'll never be good enough for you, but then nobody will." Her mouth crumples into a smile at these familiar words. "So I can't think this is a good thing, but maybe you just need to move off home base. Have a little adventure." Her face brightens, and I know this is what she was hoping to hear. "You can always come home. You can always change course. But if you want this you should go ahead and do it."

We toast our glasses, and I wonder what the hell I've just done.

In the months to come I watch her ebb and flow with the excitement of being in a new place and the eventual boredom of her job there. They move from Indiana to Colorado, and she talks about their charming community and the quaint house they've rented, until time passes and again the boredom returns.

One morning I pick up the phone and hear her sobbing. She finally spits the words out that she and her boyfriend are splitting up and she feels stuck without a car and doesn't know what to do. I keep her on the phone for over an hour talking this through, what's possible, what her next steps might be. It's a Wednesday in late August and registration at the University of Wyoming starts on Friday. With a few calls, I have her transcripts from the local community college sent to Laramie. After another call, my brother's daughter, Sarah, heads down to Colorado Springs and loads Amy up into her Subaru and drives her to Laramie to get registered and find a place of her own. With this fork in her path, a time of unfolding begins.

I turn east out of Cowley and follow my memory past sugarbeet fields and hayfields to find the cemetery. Across the entrance is a welded metal overhang, and I turn under it and park, gathering my flowers, my jacket and a small canvas bag to go in search of John Hopkin's grave. I pass the larger, older headstone of his grandfather Claude and come to a small granite slab lying flat on the fresh grave. A sheepwagon nestled in tall grass is carved to one side of the stone and across the top a horizon of mountains. A stream winds down past the camp and two evergreens, above the words

JOHN LEWIS HOPKIN

JUNE 21, 1940

OCTOBER 4, 2003

"Goddamn it, John. Where the hell have you been?" I unwrap the flowers and push them into a cup in the cement base. Given all the years he took care of the herders, tending their camps and whims, it seems unbearable to me that he was ill and passed without me knowing or helping.

I try to think of who to be mad at for not calling to tell me, but I haven't kept up with people here and can only blame myself. I only happened upon the news when I called Elaine, who ranches just north of Heart Mountain. She has family in Lovell and Cowley and takes that paper. "Damn, I missed John Hopkin's funeral last week," she'd said. "Did you go?"

"*John?* Are you sure?"

"Well, yes, it's here in the paper."

"I didn't know, never heard anything and never even saw him in these last few years after he and Charlie moved and their number was unlisted."

"I guess his friend moved away, and he was real sick the last two years. Nobody seems to know for sure what, but they say he didn't want anybody to know. Didn't seem to want anybody to find him. I think Lila kept up with him, though."

"Damn it, damn it. I had no idea."

It's now mid-October but the sun's clear and warm. I settle down next to the gravestone and pour myself a cup of coffee from the thermos, unwrap a meatloaf sandwich, and share some with Grace. She smacks her lips in protest of the ketchup but holds me in a deep stare, ready for more.

"You're one spoiled dog, you are." She whimpers hopefully in reply. "You should've known John's dog Rusty. Now he was a sheepdog. Compared to him, you're just one spoiled Australian shepherd lapdog." Her bobbed tail wiggles in the grass as she follows the meatloaf to my mouth. "Rusty only had three legs and he could put any sheep anywhere anytime." I run my hand across the gray granite, feeling the rough texture of the grass and stream and mountains carved into it. "There'll never be anyone else like him. Or like John. Never anybody in the whole world, damn him anyway."

Heart Mountain rises up all alone out of the high sagebrush desert of the Big Horn Basin to an elevation of over eight thousand feet. The Crow tribe called it Buffalo Heart Mountain, the Shoshone, Home of the Birds. To each it was a sacred place. To the eleven thousand Japanese Americans interned at its base during World War II, it was their horizon. And from anywhere I've traveled across the basin, it's been part of my horizon, too. Across Cody, it nearly casts a shadow.

On the first of May 2004, I'm hiking the Heart Mountain ridge road as I have just about every year on this day since Jenny's death five years ago. This track follows the sharp crease that curves the northern boundary of Buck Creek Basin and climbs to the double green gates at the saddle. This afternoon I only want to hike that far and look over into the north slopes of Heart Mountain, the Absaroka and Beartooth ranges beyond.

Much of the winter, winds keep this route scoured of snow, and in the spring it's the first to clear. In early May, small spring flowers are low to the ground, tucked out of the wind in among the sage; alpine phlox, shooting stars, yellow violets, wild iris. I climb the ridge, one foot in front of the other, and think about what I have come to know about this place. I've learned where the sage grouse gather each spring to drum and mate in the early frosty hours of morning. I've learned how the elk move across Skull Creek Pass to winter on the mountain and that more of them are summering, too, some say because of the wolves. I've learned to watch for a young boar grizzly who happens over to the mountain but never stays. I've learned that botanists get dewy eyed over the rare plants found here: Absaroka goldenweed, aromatic pussytoes, Howard's forget-me-nots, Shoshonea. I think about what Amy has told me, that she knows in losing her sister she's done the hardest thing she'll ever have to do and that this makes her brave. I vow to remember her words whenever I get scared or lost, because remembering them sometimes makes me fierce again.

When Grace and I reach the saddle, the wind blasts through the metal gates, straining them against the chains and playing the crossbars in wavering chords. I bury my nose in my collar and hang at the gate, determined to linger at least for a moment. From this place, I can look up the steep pitches to the top of the mountain, across the Two Dot Ranch to the west and down to Elaine's ranch in the north, where elk feed on tender new grass after last fall's burns.

From across the miles, wind howls through strands of barbed wire and draws its bow across them. I look for the sound as though in this cacophony an orchestra might be warming up, getting ready for what it's meant to do. A tumbleweed shakes loose from the fence and sails bouncing across the slopes, a note gone wild.

# CLAIMING GROUND

The sign on the airport wall says WELCOME TO GRIZZLY COUNTRY.
I've passed it a hundred times coming in and out of the Cody
airport, never giving it a glance or thinking it odd, but my parents' flight is late and I have time on my hands. I study the
large sepia photo next to it of three cowboys on horseback
pulling a small plane up a grassy hill with ropes dallied around
their saddle horns, this entitled *Backcountry Rescue*, 1938. And
farther down the wall, in a photo dated 1936, the pilot's kneel-
ing in front of the plane with twenty-three baby antelope
curled in the grass around him, destined for zoos across the

country and Europe. Above the baggage claim, among advertisements for hotels, a large poster of Heart Mountain says WELCOME TO THE BIG HORN BASIN. I wander over to the bank of windows facing the airfield and watch the night sky for signs of their plane, aware that I've been forgetting to breathe.

My mother comes through the security doors first, followed by my father, their faces scanning the small group of welcomers. I raise a hand to get their attention and watch them break into smiles. "We made it!" He's in a jaunty tweed cap and leather bomber jacket; she's in her soft traveling clothes and wearing bright lipstick and the earrings I'd given her for Mother's Day. I lean in to hug them, to welcome them, and feel them to be bright sparks, alive and awake beneath my hands. It's been over six months since we've been together, and they've come for my fiftieth birthday and, more important, for Amy's graduation from the University of Wyoming.

Getting them settled in my home, I pour small glasses of wine, and we visit before going to bed. They've brought books along, notes, and are writing articles and outlining presentations. They're deep into the conversations of an election year and worried for our country. It's late at night, later for them by two hours, and they're well into their eighties. But they are engaged by life, full of it, in a way that some people never are. The lamp's amber glow illuminates their faces, and I find myself drawing close as I would to a fire.


We're passing the Hoodoo Ranch south of town, just beginning our long drive down across the state. The morning light's strong, casting long shadows through the sagebrush. On Carter

Mountain there are pockets of snow. It's the three of us in the car, leaving Cody early in the day, a Friday, with the trunk full of coolers, tablecloths and platters of food for Amy's celebration dinner that night.

"We've brought Kentucky bourbon chocolates," my father says, "some for Amy and some for you and a box to share at the party." These dark chocolates are a family favorite, richly filled with bourbon and with a southern pecan on top, and nothing that can be found in Wyoming. "Will Amy's dad make the trip, do you suppose?"

"He says so. I saw him just last week, the first time I've seen or talked to him since the funeral. I was headed over the mountain to Sheridan and stopped at the café in Shell to gas up. He was there, in a booth, having breakfast."

My parents, astute and respectful, won't stumble into the hard places without invitation. It's silent, and I realize I'm meant to go on.

"It's been so long. He seemed glad to see me, so I sat down and had a visit. He was smiling, sunny like he always could be, still shoeing horses, though I've heard his hip's really bad. He loves her like the world and says he'll be there."

"Do they see each other much?" my mother asks.

"They're very close. They talk often, and she stays with him any time she comes north. She knows the best part of him, that sweet way he can have, his humor, his love of good books. She loves him, defends him."

After Jenny's funeral I'd called for help in unloading a stone bench at her grave but never heard back. He'd quit answering the phone, maybe only for me, though I don't think so. There are things about this man I'll never understand. But

I've come to know that there can be a time when the story's just too hard, and you have to close the book, put it back on the shelf, and walk into another room.

"Well," my dad says, "I'll be glad to see him. I'll make a point of it to visit with him and make him feel comfortable."

Driving down the road, I stumble over the question: "What is it that lets you grow old so well? Is it luck, attitude, exercise, some special vitamins?"

This sounds silly and makes all three of us laugh. But apparently they've talked about it before, and they have answers.

"Well, we try not to talk about our ailments."

"We cultivate an interest in young people and their lives. And we make an attempt to contribute where we're needed."

"And we exercise."

They finish with a flourish, as though they've made a pact and signed on the dotted line.

By comparison, my life feels haphazard, tilting, scattered and foolish. Turning fifty, I want to have a story to tell, a milestone to celebrate, but it feels like things are falling apart. My lover of several years has grown distant, distracted, tied up in knots about leaving his job. I had imagined building a house with this man, creating a life from scratch, a marriage, a story that has a plot, makes sense, and has a happy ending. Instead of loose ends getting knit together, though, I feel them unraveling day by day.

South of Thermopolis, the road cuts through blazing red cliffs in the Chugwater Formation. We begin what feels like the descent into the Wind River Canyon, but the rising walls are deceiving. The river we're following is actually flowing north, against us, headed for the Yellowstone and eventually the Missouri. We are, in fact, ascending through the canyon to the Wind River Basin and south toward Laramie.

Rising up, we drive through Sand Draw, Sweetwater Station, Jeffrey City and Muddy Gap, then pull off the highway by some gravel piles and picnic from the open trunk. The wind's whipping, so we forego paper plates and eat straight from the coolers—cheese and ham with mustard and crackers, coffee from the thermos, dark chocolate broken into pieces—and my parents rise to the occasion with light heart and a sense of adventure. We laugh that in all this open and stunning country, we've tucked ourselves up in some construction site. I watch them lean into the trunk to pour half-and-half into their coffee and think about all the places they have followed me to, from my sheep camp at the top of Burnt Mountain to the Diamond Tail Ranch on Shell Creek, from my cow camp at Granite Pass to our home on Beaver Creek, then to Greybull, Salt Lake City, and Cody. They've slept in sheep wagons, tents, hotel rooms, camper trailers, on lumpy futons, on mattresses on the floor. For weddings and funerals and birthdays they've crossed the country to be here. I've spent many years leaving them far behind, but they have always found me, and now I find myself wanting to be with them, to soak them up. This day, more than ever, I appreciate having them at my side.

As I pull the car back onto the blacktop, puffs of clouds sail by in the spring light and cast streams of shadow across the road.

My mother leans forward over the back of the seat. "So remind us of who'll be here tonight?"

"Pretty much the whole cast of characters. Amy's mother's

family will be in from Duluth, her Norwegian grandparents and her two aunts, and I believe a cousin. And from Texas, there'll be Joe's mother from the panhandle, and his brother, Ken, from San Antonio. You would've met him at the funeral."

As we visit about each one—where I'd last seen them, what they've been up to through the years—I feel my stomach tightening.

"I'm a little nervous about seeing everybody," I say, feeling myself descending the cobwebby basement steps into my past. I've lived my life by closing doors and moving on, but now I'm heading back into the deep pitch of it all. We haven't all been together in five years, since Jenny's funeral, and those memories are only of loss, numb grief and incomplete sentences.

My father reaches over and gives my shoulder a squeeze. "Well, we're right here with you."

"We're family," my mother adds, "and we'll back you up," this last part with some humor and sounding more like we're bank robbers than visitors.

Still, the words sit inside me and shore me up.


We arrive at Amy's apartment in the early afternoon, and she's glowing. Her blonde hair's cut chin-length, swingy, and she's bustling around in cropped pants and flip-flops stringing up white party lights on the patio fence. She greets us with a big hugs. "Can you believe I finally made it?"

Then her father walks through the gate, favoring one leg and wearing a white shirt and worn suede vest, his cowboy hat pulled low. Amy lights up at the sight of him and throws her arms around his neck. He gives greetings all around, leaning into each handshake with a soft, respectful voice and a shy smile.

"Fit to kill," his two brothers would say about Joe's grin. I remember him in his striped shirt and suspenders, his hat tipped back, tending to steaks on the grill with a beer in one hand, telling a story. And that grin would come after the punch line, as if to say, *Can you believe it?* His grin was a beam, an invitation to the devil, and it showed up whenever there was a song to be sung or a Texas two-step to be danced. It had been a part of the bright light shining on the early years of our marriage, but as sometimes happens, it had turned into something that represented all I couldn't bear.

"Hi, Joe," I say.

"Hello," he says back, tipping his head down in a gracious nod.

By the next morning, Joe's mother and older brother have arrived, and now all three families are gathered around Amy. In her little apartment, we scramble eggs, fry sausages and pour coffee around the room. We fill our plates and sit in folding chairs or on the floor in the living room with graduation gifts piled up like another guest. We nudge them toward her, presents from all of us, and also from friends and family who couldn't be here.

In this gathering, histories sit uneasily side by side. I watch the faces around the circle and think of the love and loss that each one holds, the memories as present as this celebration, the dead as present as the living.

Joe has been quiet, sitting on the edge of the circle with his eyes resting on Amy. It is for her that he endures the rest of us, for her that he endures me. It has been a long time since I've let myself remember him as someone I loved. As the young man who followed me to my remote camps and brought stories and laughter, the man who could build anything with a chainsaw and was the first to dance at a party and the last to leave. I loved the man who braided his daughters' hair as meticulously as he did reins and rawhide, who packed them up the mountain and out in the hills by horse or pickup to work with him day after summer day. It has been twelve years since we divorced, and since then, with only a handful of words spoken between us, the drifts of blame have piled high.

Amy opens her gifts, one by one, then stands up from where she's been sitting cross-legged on the floor and comes to each of us and gives us a hug. To each of us she says, "Thank you." To each of us she says, "I love you." She has her arms open wide, letting us, in all our imperfections, love her back.


After the graduation ceremony, we celebrate at a hip little restaurant downtown. When a tall, fair young man passes by, Amy calls him over and introduces him. They've only barely met and have yet to go on a date, which today she doesn't even know they'll do. He leans over the table and shakes the hands of friends, parents and grandparents, and I can tell that he's kind and that his mother has raised him well. "A counselor at a group home for teens," Amy says, shrugging her shoulders, but I catch a glimpse of a smile. They will have that first date and fall in love just weeks before she packs to leave Wyoming for an internship in Tucson. In two years' time they will marry in the Shell Church and dance in the community hall, but today they have no idea of this. He walks out the front door and wheels away on his bicycle.

Around the table are Joe's family, Amy's mother's family, my parents, Press with his wife and daughter, and the smart and beautiful women who have become Amy's closest friends. Toasts are made, and Joe's brother stands and raises his glass "in honor of Amy, the daughter of Joe Ed Little and Linda Ramfjord Little." I realize I shouldn't be sitting next to Amy while her father's down at the end of the table, so we switch places, awkwardly, as eyes tear up around the table at this solemn moment.

With a seven-hour drive back to Cody, Mom and Dad and I agree to slip out once the meal's over and get on the road. As we make the rounds saying good-bye, Amy's aunt comes up and gives me a big hug. "I'm sorry your sister isn't here," I tell her, *the one who should be,* I think, but don't say. At the door, Joe stands large and immobile as though ready to bolt from the concentration of people, emotion and memory. But when I extend a hand to say good-bye, he wraps me in a bear hug and says, "I don't know how to thank you for all you've done," and holds me and holds me. When he releases me, my eyes are wet with tears, and I'm the one who shoots out the door.

It's nearly midnight when my parents and I pull into Cody, the place that has become my home. I want to stand in the moonlit shadow of Heart Mountain and claim something solid and enduring. I want to *be* this mountain, but my life feels more like a hall of trick mirrors with a different view in each one.

It's my last weekend with my lover, but I don't know it yet. We have each walked through fire this spring and retreated into our own lives to make sense of it—me into writing, he into dreams of building a boat and traveling—but here we are, together again, having shed our skins. "Hello," I say brightly. "Hello!" What I notice is that we laugh more, naked and cross-legged in bed eating or making love. "What shall we do with ourselves now? Build a house? Grow a garden? Learn Spanish?" We read out loud to each other in a patch of sunlight. He is thoughtful, open, his heart coming out every pore. He massages my feet, lingering over me. He has moist eyes and the cherishing look of a man about to jump off a cliff. Then, on Sunday morning, he tells me he wants to be free to travel, to meet someone else. He kisses me good-bye and walks out the door, and I never see him again.

I find out later that he'd begun another relationship, had begun it months before. My sister gives me a copy of Pema Chödrön's *When Things Fall Apart*. A Buddhist nun, Chödrön writes that we should embrace the change, embrace the fear. When your world falls apart, there is an opportunity for gold to emerge.

But what to do about the burning coal in my chest?

I wait days before calling my parents, then call them about something else and mean to slip this news in as an aside. But then they're both on the phone with me, and when the words come out, I hear my mother gasp in surprise and outrage. And the tears come to my eyes and will not stop. My eyes closed, the phone pressed to my ear, my world becomes the sound of their voices across eighteen hundred miles saying they love me, saying I'm too good for him, saying I'm their treasure, their words overlapping each other's and choking me into tears I hadn't wanted to show, that I'd never in my life shown them. The tears that come are old tears, and I weep for the loss of Jenny, for the loss of my marriage, and for every small hurt I have hidden away in my silence and solitude. Through it all they keep talking to me. *My treasure, my love.*

For months I try in every way possible to make the betrayal not hurt. I try forgiving him, feeling sorry for him, feeling sorry for myself. I rage and contemplate breaking his windows. I declare my freedom and buy a little black dress, throw up my hands and dance. But nothing lasts for long, and as the months go by, I reluctantly bring the mirror to my face. Have I lied and hurt others with my lies? *Yes.* Have I pretended that I could step from one life to another with no consequence? *Yes.* Have I righteously chosen my own stories, discarding the ones that make me look bad? *Yes.*

Oh, I think, this is how that feels. My blame burns to ash.

I call my mother on the phone. They've booked passage on the Trans-Siberian Railway as part of their sixtieth-anniversary celebration, but my father is having last-minute hesitations because of health issues. And my mother, uncharacteristically, shares her frustration and anger. "He's *old*, and if he's old then I must be, too! I want to feel adored," she says, raging against the dying of the light. I call her back two days later, just before they're about to leave. "Mom," I say, "I adore you," but she doesn't need to hear it. They've unburdened their anger, worked it out, touched and found each other again. On the phone they both sound giddy as teens.

So this is where I've come from, I think, the good news and the bad. In their eighties, instead of shrinking they've grown larger and more fierce. The bad news? There seems to be no coasting.

This is what I'm made of. From my father I have received thoughtfulness, a love of books and dancing, the inclination to play with ideas. From my mother I have inherited the courage to leap, the ability to compete, lightheartedness, an elemental surprise at being loved.

Chödrön says that things falling apart is both a testing and a healing. We think the point is to pass the test or to overcome the problem, but the truth, she says, is that things don't really get solved once and for all. Time after time, things come together and they fall apart again, like breathing.

I remember riding through the Gravel Creek drainage eight years after the Yellowstone fires of 1988 on a ten-day pack trip that led from a trailhead west of Cody, into the Park and out the south side, toward Jackson Hole. The fires had raged in this drainage, drilling a fierce heat down into the soil that sterilized it of all life. Riding through stinging rains, we found ourselves in a world fallen apart. With no vegetation to hold the soil, cliffs had slumped into creek bottoms and water had cut raw channels through the hillsides, leaving only cobble. Even then I knew that wind-blown wisps of soil would someday catch among the gravel, that live seed would be dropped from passing birds, that in my lifetime this chaos would grow back into wild-knit life. But who among us can bear to see it go without a tear?

I'm sitting in front of the fire in a cabin that I'm house-sitting miles up Breteche Creek, west of Cody toward Yellowstone Park. It's twelve below zero this morning and snowing lightly. The lower valley is narrow and private, flanked by volcanic escarpments whose rims have been weathered into knobby pinnacles the locals call hoodoos and that lean spiritlike over the valley, keeping watch. I look the word up in the dictionary and find a negative meaning, a person or thing that brings bad luck, but in this country I've never heard it used that way. They're gnomish, ghostlike, watchful, and when the wind blows hard through the valley, there's a sound like the deep and steady vibration of the pipe organ.

Visiting my parents the past Christmas, I'd asked my father about the word *redemption*. "It's been on my mind," I say, "but I don't know what it means."

I understand this is a risk. He's a theologian and has the intellect to go on for hours, but he pauses, surveying his options, and chooses simplicity. "If you feel worthless," he says, "and someone restores your sense of value, you've been 'redeemed.' "

We're driving Kentucky's winding roads to visit with my

great-aunt, Ella, who recently turned a hundred, and to see my grandparents' graves in the Cynthiana cemetery and the tobacco farm where my mother was raised. She's in the backseat, and I'm up front, taking notes on a yellow pad.

"If you were sold into slavery," he says, "and someone has paid the price to free you, you've been redeemed. It can mean revalued," he adds, then pauses again.

I imagine him running through a list of theological references in his head. Instead, he chooses to meet me on my own ground. "The idea of redemption has meaning in terms of the work you do, in terms of conservation. You pay the price and redeem the land for future generations; the land is freed, saved."

I nod, unsure of where I was going with this question in the first place.

Nearly thirty years ago, I'd headed west to find refuge in the empty spaces of this land where I still live. Among the sage and rocks and transient lives of the herders, I hid as others might hide in heroin or alcohol. I didn't think I knew how to live in the world, and sheer miles had been my cloak from it. I look back now and realize I was lucky in my choosing, blessed beyond measure. The isolation had tossed sharp splinters of life straight back up in my face, waking me to the crack of thunder, the smell of rain that hadn't yet hit the ground. This land where I'd hidden offered up gold coins of sunlight and held me constant under a bewildering sky of stars.

In this pause of conversation, I look back and see my mother dozing with her head tilted into the window. Beside her on the seat are gardening shears and gloves, for the cleaning of her parents' graves, and also a small cooler with chicken salad for her aunt Ella. In her lap are papers for a presentation she's preparing, the pen fallen from her hand. On her sweater there's a brightly colored metal pin of three female stick figures, arm in arm, their heads haloed by ropes of wild hair.

It seems our love is never enough, by nature can *never* be enough, until you realize that it is or maybe once you decide it is. Then there it is, tender love strewn like petals at your feet, everywhere as far as you can see, thick and soft, under your feet. A place to lie down, a soft place that has always been there, but you've not seen it.

Above the cabin, Breteche valley widens into a high sagebrush bowl with clumps of aspen and conifer draws. The Breteche Creek Ranch rises up into the divide that separates the drainages of the north and south forks of the Shoshone River, its windswept spine reaching out from the heart of the Yellowstone country in a high migratory corridor that allows wolves, grizzlies, elk and bighorn sheep passage through its dark timber and bare cliffs, out through the forest and onto Sheep Mountain and the outer edges of their territory.

Several years ago, this ranch was on the market and was being bid on by a developer looking to split it up into fifty-two parcels. I'd worked to find a buyer who instead would protect it and keep it whole. In a job that often feels like I take three steps back for every step forward, this one clear shifting of fate seems an undeniable success, a celebration of my efforts to give something back.

On my last day here I walk the dirt road back up to the high basin, with chinook winds blowing up the valley and softening the snow. At the drift fence, a black cloud of crows squawking in alarm rises up from the hillside and leaves behind an intricate stitching of tracks as sharp as frost splinters, and I find a deer kill, a fresh one, the body no more than pieces exploded through the sage—tufts of hair, a hoof, a scapular bone, patches of snow stained red. It's already been picked nearly clean, and beyond the carnage in the clean white snow, there are coyote tracks, many of them.

The only thing that remains intact is the intestine—or rather its contents, lying on the snow in the perfect shape of that organ. I know the deer's winter browse must be sage leaves, willow tips, wildrye, fescue and bluebunch wheatgrass, but I can't tell much by looking. I see only brown shredded plant matter closely compacted into the graceful shape of a bota bag full of wine. What's amazing is that the intestine walls are simply picked clean, leaving only the contents. I imagine a magician pulling a tablecloth from a fully set table without disturbing the candelabra and place settings.

I find a rock to sit on in the sun next to the fence beside the kill. Grace quits her nosing around to come and sit by me, looking to my eyes as if to ask what it is, exactly, that we're searching for. We sit there watching for something to show a face. From atop the hoodoo ridges, crows caw. A golden eagle dips a wing in a slow glide above them. There must be eyes watching us from the pockmarks in the volcanic cliffs, but I can't see them. The sun's warm, all is quiet, and we simply sit there listening to the birds.

I'm aware that standing up and leaving means going back

to the tangle of my life, giving up the spacious silence of these days. When a cloud passes over and it grows cold, I pull my coat around my neck and look one last time at the scattered bones and bloodstains on the hillside, thinking we all have our time of reckoning. If we're lucky, there's something left of us to persist. And if we're supple of heart, we get to gather our bones together and walk on in the world with our noses to the wind, bright eyed for the days ahead.

## ACKNOWLEDGMENTS

I extend my love and deepest appreciation to the following people, whose lives appear along with mine in these pages: Virginia and Wayne Bell, Amy Little Bey, Joe Ed Little, Ken Little, Nadyne Little, Stan and Mary Flitner, Tim Flitner, Carol Flitner Bell, Sonia Jensen, Gretel Ehrlich, Lila Steed, Paul Schmidt, John McGough, Press Stephens, and my siblings, Kendall Bell, David Bell, Marsha Uselton and Brenda Bell. You have made my life and story rich.

My thanks go to Page and Pearre' Williams for the months I spent upstream in their Breteche Creek cabin and to Anne Young for timely seclusion in her cabin at Moss Creek. For encouragement and logistical support, I want to thank my family, my wide scatter of friends, the Louises, David Beckett, Harriet Corbett, Emily Milder and the staff at Knopf, the Ucross Foundation, Neltje and the Blanchan/Doubleday Literary Awards, the Wyoming Arts Council and my colleagues at the Wyoming Chapter of the Nature Conservancy.

I thank Joe Little for giving his blessing to the manuscript, an act of love and courage.

I am grateful to Mark Spragg for his generous support for my voice, to Virginia Spragg for her dedicated, insightful, and unflagging reads of this manuscript, and to my agent, Nancy Stauffer, for her patience and care.

With a handful of sentences, my editor, Gary Fisketjon, turned me toward a steeper path, and I am forever in his debt.

I raise a toast to Jenny Little, Linda Ramfjord Little, John Lewis Hopkin, Grady Steed, Fred Murdi and my dogs, Louise, Lady and Grace. May they all rest in peace together on the big mountain.